What People are Saying About *Creating Generational Wealth*®

"All middle class Americans need to read this book. Because US tax, legal and economic issues are quite complicated and often confusing. But Mr. Eze simply explains the financial information we all need to know, in a step by step, easy to understand process that will enable us to save, grow and protect our money—not only for ourselves, but for our children and grandchildren too."

Dan Viñal
President, WebPrez, LLC

"Douglas, thank you for sharing the wisdom that helps so many create generational wealth. Applying the principles you have taught has provided a paradigm for the financial future of my family. Your economic aptitude is evidence of your faith for wealth building success. This book will challenge you to change and experience wealth building breakthroughs."

Bishop Jason L. Brownlee
Life Changing Christian Center, White Plains, MD

CREATING GENERATIONAL WEALTH®

Kim
To your wealth
legacy, keep
changing lives

CREATING GENERATIONAL WEALTH®

What the Super Wealthy Know that You Need to Know

DOUGLAS A. C. EZE

PUBLISHED BY LARGO FINANCIAL SERVICES

Creating Generational Wealth®: What the Super Wealthy Know that You Need to Know

Published by Largo Financial Services
6401 Golden Triangle Drive, Suite 115
Greenbelt, MD 20770

ISBN: 978-0-9899515-0-0

Copyright © 2013 by Douglas Anthony Chukwuka Eze

All rights reserved. No part of this book may be reproduced or transmitted in any form or by any means, electronic or mechanical, including photocopying and recording, or by any information storage and retrieval system, without permission in writing from the publisher.

Legal disclaimer: The material presented in this book is for informational purposes. While care has been taken to present the concepts in an accurate and updated fashion, the author makes no expressed or implied warranty of any kind and assumes no responsibility for errors or omissions. No liability is assumed for incidental or consequential damages in connection with or arising out of the use of the information contained here.

Cover photo: Jackie Hicks, Fond Memories Photography
Cover and interior design: Adina Cucicov, Flamingo Designs

ACKNOWLEDGMENTS

First, I would like to thank the Almighty Father for protecting and guiding me throughout my life.

To my parents: the late Chief Godwin Eze and my mother, Cordelia Eze. I also want to thank my sister Uzoamaka Okosieme, my brother Iyke Eze, and my late brother, Pastor Godwin Eze, all of whom supported me in my efforts to reach the dreams of our family. Your encouragement has carried me through many days, weeks, months, and years; I know our efforts will benefit many more generations of the Eze legacy.

The following leaders have been instrumental in my personal, professional, and business development:

- Dr. Roger F. Salter, Founder and CEO of Sanmar Financial Network
- Pastor Tom Donkor, Higher Heights International Church
- Sam Liang, CEO of Rubino and Liang, LLC
- Dr. Gabriel Dada, Pastor of Christ Apostolic Church (Tampa)
- Leland Landes, The Legacy Group, Inc.
- Donald L. Blanton, Owner and President of Money*Trax*, Inc.

Creating Generational Wealth®

To all of the agents who have worked with me and supported me in developing and sustaining Largo Financial Services, Inc. and to my American Classic Agency family, especially the Policastro and Segal families, I thank you.

To everyone who has been a blessing in my life and helped me become the man that I am today, you know who you are—I thank you.

DEDICATION

To my lovely wife Chinyere Eze and my children Kelvin James Chukwuka Meehan and Adaora Ngozi Eze—this book is for you.

My journey started at the age of 17 when I first had the vision of traveling across the ocean to an opportunity I had never seen but knew in my heart existed. Now, more than 20 years later, I am on the path to fulfilling this dream. No matter what, never give up on your dreams.

I also dedicate this book as a guide for generations to come to my grandchildren and great grandchildren. I want all of you to benefit from the fruits of my labor while understanding the journey of creating wealth was not an easy journey.

TABLE OF CONTENTS

Foreword 1
Introduction: Who is Douglas Eze? 3
Chapter 1: The World Of Personal Finance 11
Chapter 2: The Wealth Gap 17
Chapter 3: Protecting Your Assets 23
Chapter 4: Estate Planning 29
Chapter 5: Owning a Business 37
Chapter 6: Owning Real Estate 47
Chapter 7: Your Wealth Legacy 51
Chapter 8: Life Insurance: The Key To Building Your Family
    Wealth Legacy 65
Chapter 9: Creating Generational Wealth with the Right Policies 73
Chapter 10: David's Story 83
Chapter 11: David and Lisa's Life 97
Chapter 12: A Conversation with the Author 107
Appendix: Key Terms & Definitions 115
Additional Resources 129
Special Recognition 131

FOREWORD

Creating Generational Wealth® is a road map for creating your own legacy while providing for your loved ones, yet it accomplishes much, much more for the reader and the practitioner.

In our world of entrepreneurship, the playing field is equal. However, one must be driven, continually self-educated, motivated from within and possess the highest integrity. In my position over the years, I have witnessed numerous individuals seeking career opportunities as well as the countless clients they endeavored to serve. Douglas Eze's achievements, the lives he has helped by teaching, those who have aspired to follow in his career footsteps, and those clients who have gained peace of mind through their determination to either turn things around or build upon what they have attained, are giving us all cause for optimism. Now, with this book, Douglas imparts what he has learned from his tireless studies and hands on techniques which he reiterates in daily practice.

The book is a mirror reflecting the life and times of its author, Douglas Anthony Chukwuka Eze. His story understates the

American opportunity by briefly and modestly tracing the steps of an African immigrant who leaves home all alone to venture to Canada then forges his way to the United States of America. This «can do self-help while helping others» book sets forth the journey of a very young independent man, ingrained with strong family values and goals who was and is determined to make a more secure and enriched life for all within his family, associates, and extended family and thus attain the American Dream.

When writer James Truslow Adams coined the phrase "the American Dream" in 1931, he described it as "That dream of a land in which life should be better and richer and fuller for everyone, with opportunity for each according to ability or achievement." The American Dream is all about opportunity demonstrated by unparalleled decades of proven success. The book is set at a time in history when the so called "American Dream" and its accompanying opportunity have been perceived as taking hit after hit. Many in Middle America believe opportunity has largely disappeared amid a poor job market, heavy debts, and wages that have stalled for 25 years.

In the midst of this despair, along comes Douglas Eze with a pillar of hope. Made in America is for all and is alive and well. Regardless of your personal journey, if you are principled and driven to Dream Big and Work Hard by following this road map, the creation of your legacy will begin.

Jerry Policastro
President and CEO
American Classic Agency

Introduction

WHO IS DOUGLAS EZE?

When I was a young man growing up in Nigeria, my father made sure my mother and siblings had the things we needed in life. He worked very hard to take care of us, even during the Nigerian Civil War when he was a member of the military. When the war ended, he retired and became a very successful businessman who owned a tractor-trailer company with six Mercedes Benz tractors.

At the time, as with many transport businesses in Africa, the drivers often damaged property and stole from the owners by doing their own side deals. These activities continued for years in my father's business until he decided to sell all his trucks and reinvest in a fashion design business while helping other family members. Essentially, he never invested his money. He never purchased stocks. He never bought any land or owned a house, and he never even thought to get a life insurance policy. The one thing my father did right was push my siblings and me to obtain a college education, offering money to those of us who made it to college.

My older siblings went to college. During that time, I was not wise with money although I hate to admit it. I treated my father's money as if it was my own and used it to hang out with my friends and go out. I was literally blowing through thousands of dollars. One day, I realized the money would not be there forever.

I do not know why I did not realize this sooner because, in Nigeria, I witnessed the same tragic story play out repeatedly. So many successful business owners, like my father, would retire only to find themselves with no money and no real assets. Even those who owned land, stocks, and real estate were unsuccessful in passing on anything of value to their families. Five years after they passed, everything they had acquired vanished because they failed to have a plan in place that would enable them to transition their wealth responsibly.

In other words, those who are rich are financially well off for a short amount of time. Those who are truly wealthy pass their wealth to their families and create a wealth legacy. When I came to the United States, I saw families who had businesses very similar to my father's, but the difference was that they had planned properly and passed these empires to their children, thus building generational wealth.

Who is Douglas Eze?

As much as I love and respect my father's memory and appreciate all of his efforts, I do not want to go down the same path. I want to properly plan for the future and ensure that my children have long-term financial stability and, ideally, generational wealth will be passed down to their children. My first step was leaving Africa.

I came to America when I was 24-years-old—still a kid really—searching for something more. I knew America was the land of opportunity and wanted to have opportunities my parents did not have. Naturally, I wanted my own children to eventually have the opportunities I did not have so their children would not struggle financially, and I would not allow them to blow through money without understanding the consequences of such irresponsible behavior. With each new generation, there is an opportunity to create generational wealth and/or an opportunity to pass down knowledge so that the new generation doesn't replicate the same mistakes of the previous generation.

When I arrived in the United States from Nigeria via Canada, I was desperately in need of work. A friend offered me a job at IHOP, and I took the opportunity. Shortly after, while I was serving a family their breakfast, a young boy walked up to me and handed me a card, explaining that his grandmother, Lorraine Manuel, wanted me to have it. I hesitantly approached the boy's grandmother, unsure of what to make of the situation. Lorraine invited me to her office for an interview the following day. That day changed my life forever, and it never would have happened if I hadn't worked at IHOP. It's funny how things work out, isn't it?

The next day, Lorraine introduced me to the financial services industry. She saw something in me that made her believe I would be successful in the industry; she was right. Looking back, I know Lorraine was instrumental in teaching me the fundamentals of this industry. Though our paths only crossed for two years before I decided to move on, those two years were pivotal in my career and learning process.

I left Lorraine with a unique vision, realizing my passion for the industry. I needed to grow and explore my potential and was ready to expand my horizons. I went to work for a number of large companies before deciding to start my own firm in 1999. I could neither attain the success I wanted working for others nor focus on what I believed to be important while fulfilling someone else's vision, so going off on my own made the most sense.

The issue was that people in the financial services industry have been programmed to *not* think outside of the box; oftentimes, it's to the detriment of their clients. At companies I worked for, I saw agents sell their clients products they did not need or products not suited for their needs, which was not the kind of environment I wanted to work in. This occurs because most insurance companies employ agents and make them a captive sales force, which means those agents can only sell the products offered by those companies. I am not about pushing products down clients' throats; I am an individual thinker and agent, which is why I had trouble working within this format.

Also, I noticed there was a misconception that people in middle America should just want to get by rather than create long-term financial security for themselves and their families. I really began to think critically about the idea of creating generational wealth. Wealth does not just have to be inherited; it can be created and passed down to benefit future generations. That being said, starting my own company was not a decision that came easily.

Let me rewind. In 1998, I was working with someone at an insurance company who was not only stealing from me, but also stealing my agents. I got to the point where I was sick and tired of being ripped off. I began to question whether or not any ethical people were in the business. One day, while I was speaking to a friend about it, he introduced me to a company called American Classic Agency (ACA). I interviewed with Mike Curtis who, like Lorraine Manuel, would prove to be instrumental to my success—a true game changer. Immediately, I knew this was an organization I wanted to build a future with.

I joined ACA in 1999. Most agents want to work for a well known company because if you are independent, you do not have a company backing you, so you do not have the luxury of benefiting from their brand recognition. However, my clients really pushed me to forge my own path. So many of them would tell me the reason they worked with me was because they trusted me, not because I had an established, recognized company behind me. I realized starting my own company was truly an option. Yes, it was scary, but change is always scary.

Because of my great rapport with Mike Curtis and the type of innovative firm ACA is, I was able to open my own company, Largo Financial Services, Inc., in 2000 as an independent organization that operates within the American Classic Agency franchise like a company. This arrangement allows me to operate independently and create my own brand while benefitting from a strategic partnership with ACA.

Since Largo Financial Services launched, my commitment to this industry has only grown. I am truly passionate about educating my clients and making a difference in the lives of working class Americans, African American communities, and other minority groups who are often left out of the generational wealth conversation. Often, they are not given the information or tools needed to learn how to manage their money, create their own wealth, and transfer that wealth from one generation to another.

While growing up in Nigeria, I often wondered how the rich stayed wealthy. In Nigeria, everyone I knew who had money eventually ran out of money, having nothing to pass to their children. My father is the perfect example. He died in his 70s while living with me in Maryland; I was taking care of him financially. My father had nothing left from his previous successful business in Africa. When he passed, it was $12,000 just to fly him back to our homeland. If my father had simply had a life insurance policy, it would have made his passing so much less stressful.

In the United States, I learned the phrase "old money." I would hear, "That person comes from old money." At the time, I did not understand what that meant, but eventually I learned it meant inherited wealth. America has family dynasties where the wealth continues to grow from one generation to the next, as was the case with the Kennedys, the Vanderbilts, and so many others.

I began to research, trying to figure out how Americans were able to not only sustain their wealth, but make it grow for each generation. I discovered there was something each of these wealthy families had in common, something I will detail in these pages. The tips and techniques you will learn in this book will help you create sustainable wealth that will benefit your family for years to come. I have taught these techniques in homes, churches, schools, and seminars; so many people have had an "aha moment." Soon, you will have yours.

Obviously, we all go to work each day not just to survive and pay the bills, but to provide a better life to our children than we had. No matter our background, economic status, race, gender, ethnicity, or religious beliefs, our common thread is a desire to make the lives of the next generation easier, happier, and better. What stops many of us from passing on financial stability is not a lack of desire, but a lack of knowledge. Eighty percent of Americans do not have the information they need to create financial stability or generational wealth. The core of my passion is a burning desire to assist families in their ultimate dream of leaving something behind for their children and grandchildren, something that will help them build the lives of their dreams and continue a legacy of knowledge and generational wealth.

As a licensed insurance agent and securities representative for nearly two decades, I am committed to helping families achieve their financial dreams. I am the founder and CEO of Largo Financial Services, an American Classic Agency National marketing director and boardroom member, and an agency recruiter and trainer.

To date, I have recruited and trained more than 2,000 insurance and financial advisors nationwide. My company has more than 600 active representatives in offices all over the country, and we are still growing. When you finish this book, you will walk away with a better understanding of how finances work, and hopefully, you will understand why I love what I do and why I have been successful at it. It's not about money; it's about helping people do better for their families.

What is YOUR Wealth Legacy?

Your *Wealth Legacy* determines the level of financial freedom you and your family have now, in the future, and for generations to come.

Chapter 1

THE WORLD OF PERSONAL FINANCE

entering the world of finance can feel scary and for good reason. The choices you make can affect your livelihood and the livelihood of your family. Without a clear understanding of growth rates and averages, you may feel confused and overwhelmed. This book has been written to serve as a trusted friend, one that can give you understanding and help coax you through the more difficult questions you will be faced with. It's like having your very own personal financial advisor in your pocket, one that can serve as your reference guide to the world of finance.

You may wonder why I have chosen to focus on creating wealth rather than getting rich. Technically, the two words mean the same thing, but the difference is being smart and intentional about how you manage your money. You can win the lottery tomorrow and spend the money on material things; however, when that money is gone, it's gone. Being wealthy means your money will grow and continue to benefit your family for years to come. In my opinion, being "rich" is shortsighted because the money is often short-lived. Think of all the celebrities, the child stars, or "have-beens" we have read about who failed to invest or manage their money properly. At one time, they were rich, yet it was fleeting. In other words, being rich is like instant gratification while being wealthy is like prolonged pleasure.

Some people, like the Walton family of Wal-Mart fame or the three brothers originally behind the Johnson & Johnson brand, are born into money while others, like Oprah Winfrey, come from poverty and obtain wealth through hard work over the course of their careers. How these people obtained their wealth now matters less than how they maintain it.

If you are reading this book to find tips on getting rich quickly, you have picked up the wrong book. I understand that many who will read these words are working class people who were not born into wealth and most likely do not have much in the way of wealth right now. The long-term goal we explore in this book is getting to a point where you feel financially stable; we want you to get to the point where, should something happen to you, it will not leave your family in debt. We want you to get to the point that your family will not struggle once you are gone, nor will they lose anything you have acquired in your lifetime, no matter how small or significant that is.

Of course, we are also trying to ensure that while you may not have had a lot during your lifetime, you make smart financial decisions that will put your family in a good position so that if they use the knowledge you acquired and decisions you made, they can begin to create the generational wealth we have been discussing. The good news is it's never too late. If you can read these words and follow my advice, you can put a plan into action that can drastically change the course of your family's life and financial wellbeing.

Creating wealth is like raising a child: it's not something that happens overnight, and you certainly will have a lifetime responsibility on your hands. You may choose to be actively involved, or you may choose to just let it find its own way. Obviously, children turn out the best when they are closely supervised and cared for; the same could be said of creating wealth. Your wealth will grow more steadily under a watchful eye.

You will need to set clear boundaries and consistently enforce them. Questions will arise that you do not know the answers to; just as this situation occurs in parenting, you will have to seek guidance and do your own research to ensure you are taking the right steps for you and your family. The end goal, of course, is to leave a legacy of financial stability and fiscal responsibility so that your children and grandchildren do not have to experience the difficulties and limitations you may have endured.

When I lecture to local communities, so many people voice similar concerns. They feel time is running out, so creating wealth for their families is no longer an option for them. So many people have the same, nagging concerns. They worry about whether or not their retirement will be enough, how they will continue to care for their families after retirement, their lack of equity, and the amount they are being taxed. These are legitimate fears. Though the concern you have failed your family is a common one, you *have* to know it is never too late to get on track financially.

Understanding how personal finance works and learning how to properly manage your money and plan for your future is not something that will just benefit you. Think of the power of being able to pass this information to your children, saving them from having to learn these lessons the hard way as so many of us have had to do. The problem is that so many families fail to openly discuss finances. As a result, many of us are taught to keep our nose to the grindstone and hope for the best. We tell our children to go to school, get a good job, and take care of their families. For many, that means living paycheck-to-paycheck. You have the power now to save your children from that fate.

A great example of following a positive financial model set by a parent is legendary American industrialist John D. Rockefeller, who learned an important lesson from his mother: to put away a small percentage of every check that comes in. When Rockefeller got his first job, he put away ten percent of everything he made. Even though he was struggling financially, he had enough money to take advantage of opportunities as they arose, enabling him to become the mega wealthy philanthropist he eventually evolved into.

Another lesson to take from this is: if you do not have even a small nest egg, how can you take advantage of great financial opportunities to invest in companies or stocks that could very well change the direction of your family's financial future? As we all know, the bank does not lend us money when we need it the most, so having the means to invest in something is also a large part of being able to create generational wealth.

There may be those of you who think you are doing better financially than you truly are. You have invested in some stocks, you have purchased some real estate, you have a company that you believe you can pass down to your children, but are you really worth as much as you think?

There is someone else interested in your wealth accumulation: Uncle Sam, who is hanging around waiting to administer a hefty fine when your kids inherit your business and property. Almost 150 years ago, the Internal Revenue Service (IRS) was created during the American Civil War to initially pay for the expenses of war, but as the organization evolved, its true purpose became clear: to make money when Americans work and when Americans open businesses. You should basically think of the IRS as your silent business partner. You have to consider that business partner every time you make a financial decision of any kind.

You probably do not realize the countless ways Uncle Sam can reach into your finances. You do your part by working hard and building your version of the American dream. Maybe you have reached out to advisors, but they are limited to setting up plans designed by the companies they work for. You did not realize you would need a good tax attorney because you were unaware of the kinds of problems your family would face when you were no longer around to run the family business. You need to have a firm understanding of how the IRS works and what it's entitled to take.

The first step is understanding that you will never escape the IRS. The moment you start a business, you are no longer a regular civilian. You can't get your taxes done at H&R Block like your friends or neighbors. Entering the world of finance means learning to operate within the IRS's framework. Although I can provide tips on what to ask and what you should know, I am not a tax attorney or advisor. As a matter of fact, the best advice I can offer is recommending that you contact a tax advisor or attorney, especially if you have a business. If you are not properly incorporated and something happens to you, your life's work and savings can go to the IRS rather than your family; clearly, this is what we are trying to avoid.

In upcoming chapters, I will discuss specific instances in which you should consult with an attorney and specific questions you should ask.

Chapter 2

THE WEALTH GAP

As I mentioned in the introduction, one of my biggest passions—and the thing I love most about the work I do—is educating working and middle-class Americans about the financial services industry and rules to the money game. The reason I believe this is so important is because too often, those communities are not taught how to financially plan for their futures. We know how to survive financially, but we do not know how to thrive and that MUST change. You can never be fully empowered and independent unless you know how to make your money work for you. By extension, you cannot be successful in creating generational wealth if you do not have a firm understanding of financial basics.

In 2012, the Census revealed that whites had about 22 times the wealth of African-Americans and 15 times the wealth of Latinos. The same report also found that in an African American household considered high-income, the average amount of assets owned is $18,000. A white household from a similar socioeconomic background owns an average of $74,000 in assets.

There is also the gender wage gap. Despite the passage of the Equal Pay Act in 1963 and the 2009 Lilly Ledbetter Fair Pay Act, women still earn only 72 percent as much as their male counterparts. In other words, for every $1 a man earns, a woman earns just 72 cents. It goes without saying that these numbers become even more dismal for women of color. To illustrate this point, take this sobering fact into account: according to the study *Lifting As We Climb: Women of Color, Wealth, and America's Future (Insight, 2010)*, the average net worth of single white women between the ages of 36-49 is $42,600. The average net worth of single women of color in the same age group: $5. It is believed that the passage of the Paycheck Fairness Act—which has been introduced to Congress twice and rejected both times—would improve these dismal numbers, but the fact remains that women of color would still be making a disproportionate amount to white women in similar fields.

The way that debt and poverty get perpetuated isn't that much of a surprise: the lack of household wealth compounds over time, from generation to generation. So, kids who come from families without much wealth take on debt to pay for basics, such as automobiles and college, so they often acquire more debt in college by obtaining credit cards with very high interest rates. While those who come from more affluent backgrounds spend their 20s and 30s making and saving money, those who do not come from wealthy or even financially stable backgrounds, spend the same time period servicing debts.

For years, countless policy makers believed home ownership might be the way to tackle the wealth gap because so much household wealth is tied to people's homes. The rationale was that getting more people to own homes could spur wealth creation. Unfortunately, quite the opposite turned out to be true.

Let's lay it all out: the middle class is disappearing. A recent paper by Brookings Institution found that poorer families are not moving up the socioeconomic scale; their disadvantages are actually growing. Economists say that the wealth gap is not only permanent, but it will continue to widen as the nation's population continues to diversify. If this is the scenario we find ourselves in and there's nothing we can do to change it, how on Earth can we fight it?

Information and education! As writer Dr. Maya Angelou says, "When you know better, you do better." This chapter is important because you have to know what you are up against. You must have a firm understanding of the structures that oppress you and hinder your financial stability.

I'd like to think that picking up this book is your first step to doing better. I am not saying I have all the answers or that following my advice will put an end to the wealth gaps, but as an immigrant who found himself in a foreign land, I had to learn the rules of the money game the hard way. I had to start from scratch, building a life and career in a country I was unfamiliar with so that my future children would be taken care of no matter what.

Despite the challenges I have faced, I consider myself fortunate. So many immigrants never secure financial stability for themselves or their children. So much of what I have accomplished was through hard work, but I also feel blessed and because of that, it is important to me to pass on what I know with the hope that it will change lives.

I also think the discussions this book presents are crucial because so often, I work with low- and middle-income communities; as we have learned in this chapter, the chips are stacked against them. Oftentimes, traditional financial institutions decline loan requests from people in those communities, which is why I advocate so strongly for establishing your own personal private reserve account with living benefits because they can serve as your private bank. It is vitally important for us to be self-reliant, no longer relying on systems in place that all too often inhibit us from generating wealth. When you have your private reserve account—or your "private bank"—your dreams do not have to be put on hold. I will talk in-depth about this concept later in the book.

So much of what I share comes from my own personal experience. For example, after my wife and I decided it was time for her to become her own boss, we decided she should leave her job at a major hospital due to all the bureaucracy. We decided it was time for her to *own* the corporate ladder instead of working for other people. We opened our own medical clinic and considered doing what most Americans do when starting a business: apply for a loan. If it were not for my "private reserve bank," we would have had to depend on a traditional financial institution to make the final decision about whether or not we could have pursued a lifelong dream. My wife would have had to put her life and career on hold until that institution gave us the green light after subjecting us to a lengthy process and who knows how long it would have taken to get a yes or no answer. We decided to go with a solution that would give us a guaranteed "yes" with no credit check, no asset reviews, no financial documents to provide and an unstructured loan repayment option.

This book has the potential to change your family's financial future and create generational wealth if your family plays its cards right, which is why education and information are so important. You may not have a lot of money to start, but if you can pass the knowledge you obtain from this book down to your children and grandchildren, if you can help them make smart financial decisions and understand crucial information about the racial wealth gap and income disparities—two things that greatly impact their lives—there will be no end to the legacy you leave behind.

Chapter 3
PROTECTING YOUR ASSETS

What will happen to all of the things you have worked so hard for when you stop working? My goal is to teach you how to protect the fruits of your labor.

If you are like most people I have met in my 15 years of doing business, you have probably never had a discussion with your family about finances or how things should work once you pass. Understandably, it is an uncomfortable conversation, but one that is so crucial to your family's wellbeing.

In the African American community, it is common for the sole breadwinner to not have a will or family trust. If you are the sole breadwinner and do not have a will or family trust, you have some very big decisions to make. In the next chapter, we will discuss the benefits of a trust over a will. Until then, take a look at the following questions because your answers will provide insight into where you are and what immediate steps need to be taken moving forward so that your estate does not end up getting contested in probate court should something happen to you unexpectedly.

1. Do you have a will?
2. Have you established a trust?
3. Do you own a business? If so, have you formed separate legal entity?
4. Do you own any real estate?
5. Do you have children?
6. Do you own a private reserve account for you and your spouse?
7. Do you have a private reserve account for each of your children?

Let's breakdown some of these questions...

Establishing whether or not you have a will or trust is at the top of the list because if something happens to you, these documents will be deferred to when dividing your assets. If neither exists, your business, property, or other assets of any kind can be contested and potentially taken away from their rightful inheritors.

If you have assets—including your home, accounts, and real estate—you should consider having a will or trust in place. The reason is simple: you have worked very hard to accumulate what you have and when you pass away, you want to make sure your assets remain in your family. Obviously, this is key in creating generational wealth, but it is also just good business.

Transferring a business to a loved one is a bit trickier than dividing your assets among your loved ones, which brings us to the next important question: is your business a separate legal entity? I have seen it so many times in my career: a family loses a loved one's business because it was not a separate legal entity and the estate taxes were so high that the family could not afford to pay them. In essence, selling the business becomes more feasible than keeping it.

The truth is that being a separate legal entity can result in a more advantageous, affordable tax situation and provide more tax benefits for business owners, which is just one of many reasons why you should consider consulting with a CPA or an attorney regarding your business formation.

Let's start with the basics. What does forming a separate legal entity mean? Essentially, it means that your company is viewed as a legal entity in the eyes of the law. This means that the company can file lawsuits, sell property, buy property, be taxed, and yes, even commit crimes! Forming certain legal entities is crucial to you because it also means that your business protects you from personal liability, company obligations, and debts within certain limits.

As a legal entity, your business will be viewed and treated separately from you. So, if your company fails, the shareholders will only lose the amount of the purchase price of their original shares. Obviously, if you are the sole shareholder, you are the only one suffering the financial loss.

As we discussed in chapter one, the IRS always gets its share. So, while we have talked about how becoming a separate legal entity can be beneficial to you from a tax perspective, do not assume that your company will not be taxed. For example, a C-corporation is taxed at two levels: for the corporate entity and at the shareholder level where shareholders are taxed on dividends received. The idea is to pay your share and nothing above that, which is something a tax attorney or CPA can help you with.

Becoming incorporated requires filing the Articles of Incorporation in your state, along with other forms. The Articles of Incorporation is a document you will file with the Secretary of State. Once this is completed, your state will issue a Certificate of Incorporation that legally entitles your business to operate.

When filing, you have to provide the following basic information for most states, although specific requirements may vary:

- The purpose of your corporation;
- Your name, address, and the names and addresses of any other incorporators;
- The type and amount of capital stock your corporation will be authorized to issue; and
- The privileges and rights of any and all stockholders.

It may seem like a lot of work, but it is worth the investment required to establish a separate legal entity. Keep in mind that the tax benefits are one common motivation for many business owners to invest the time and money—because it costs money—

to create a separate legal entity for their companies. That being said, let's look at two other reasons why you might specifically consider incorporation:

- Unlike other legal structures, such as a sole proprietorship or partnership, the life of your corporation will not be dependent on your life. Remember, we are talking about creating generational wealth. Once that entity has been formed, your business can continue until it accomplishes a specific goal, merges with another company, is sold, or goes bankrupt. In other words, it can go on indefinitely and, if you take the appropriate steps as we have been discussing, it can exist within your family for many years, accomplishing your goal of creating generational wealth.

- Keeping with our overall creating generational wealth theme, having shares of your business that are easily transferrable is another major bonus of becoming incorporated. With your corporation, ownership interest can be easily sold, transferred, or given away to another family member. With corporations, your shares represent your rights and privileges. You may quickly and efficiently transfer business ownership by simply signing the back of each stock certificate. To bring this full circle, if you are personally unable to transfer the stocks, your attorney could refer to your trust for instructions for handling the transaction.

Question number four is, "Do you own real estate?" If you do, it becomes even more crucial for you to work with an estate planning attorney who can advise you on how to manage your real estate within your will and/or trust. We will discuss estate planning in more detail in the next chapter.

Chapter 4

ESTATE PLANNING

When it comes to estate planning, you have to look at everything you have, including your house, bank accounts, insurance policies, and anything else you think may count as an asset. Again, this may be a good time to utilize an expert, such as a board certified estate planning attorney, who will provide advice including how to:

- Establish a trust; and/or
- Prepare a will.

Why is this important? If you are at all concerned about protecting your assets and/or preventing your heirs from having to pay additional money after your death due to liability or taxes, meeting with an estate planning attorney is the best solution to determine the approach that works for you. Many families have been left in turmoil because a deceased loved one left an unexpected financial burden. Is that really how you want your family to remember you?

The only thing we know in life is that we will die. We do not know when, but the important question is whether or not we will be prepared once it happens.

What is the difference between a trust and a will?
Both wills and trusts reflect how you desire to have your inheritance managed—who receives what, when they receive it, and how it is received.

"For those who are concerned with their privacy and avoiding probate, a trust is preferred," says Florida attorney Joseph Pippin. Attorney Pippin, who specializes in estate planning, provided this excellent distinction between wills and trusts.

Estate Planning

Trust/Will Differences

Q. What is the difference between having a will and having a trust?
A. I commonly use the following chart to help people understand the difference between wills and trusts.

WILLS	TRUSTS
Probate costs—3-10%	Probate costs—0
Time of probate—6 to 14 months	Time of probate—0
Guardianship planning—NO	Guardianship planning—YES
Privacy of affairs—NO	Privacy of affairs—YES

Explanation

Probate costs: Attorney's fees range from 3% to 10% of the estate. Personal representatives (i.e. executors) are also entitled to a fee.	Trust assets do not go through probate. Thus, you save the attorney's fee and the executor's fee.
Time: Probate usually takes from 6 to 12 months and sometimes much longer.	Trust assets may be distributed without attorney and court involvement and therefore can be distributed much faster.
Guardianship Planning: Wills are instruments that give instructions upon death. Wills do not do anything for guardianship planning.	Your trust names someone who can manage your affairs upon your incapacity without a court appointed guardian. This could save a substantial amount of time and money in guardianship fees.
Privacy: Upon death, wills are recorded and the public may review or buy copies of them. The public may also buy copies of deeds, mortgages, lawsuits, etc. Therefore, wills are a matter of public record.	Trusts generally do not have to be recorded; thus the public does not know the contents of the document.

Living trusts should be considered by all persons whose total estate exceeds $75,000

Source: Joseph Pippen (www.attypip.com)

A living trust will not become part of the public record unless a trustee or a beneficiary demands court approval of accounts. Probate records are always open to the public.

Just to give you an idea: remember legendary, rugged movie star John Wayne? The star died in 1979, but his children are still battling over his will in probate court! Let's be clear: trusts are sometimes contested as well, but it can be more difficult to do. Trusts can be much more complicated because of how extensively you can specify your wishes for your estate.

Again, when establishing your trust, you will want to consult an expert. If you are clear about your mission of creating generational wealth, then you will want to be clear with your attorney about how to prepare your money, interests, and assets for the time when you can no longer manage them yourself. Be clear about instructions for how business should be conducted on your behalf as well as the message and legacy you leave behind for your family.

Speak with your personal tax advisor or attorney about the details that will affect your estate's taxability. In some instances, you may even have to pay taxes after your death! Remember, the IRS is around every corner; just as you had to pay them while alive, your estate may have to pay after your death. Some state and federal estate taxes can be as high as 55 percent.

The good news is that a trust can help shield your assets from being consumed by the IRS. Your family trust will provide protection from those lurking to find your money to claim for themselves when you are no longer around to defend it. What often happens once a person passes is some people come out of the woodwork attempting to claim a piece of the pie. As mentioned previously, a trust enables you to outline exactly who gets what in terms of your assets, including your business. Clearly, this is particularly useful from a business perspective, as it allows you to control your business from the grave.

Your family trust may become the beneficiary of your 401(k) plan, if you have one. It may also own your property and any other assets you might have. This is referred to as funding your trust. Because your assets are owned by the trust, you may increase the inheritance you pass on by helping your children avoid a huge gift tax. This is another great reason to consult with a board certified estate planning attorney.

The major problem in many cases of family business transfers is they tend to be inadequate for estate planning. Many parents assume a successful business transfer is assured as long as their wills specify how the assets should be split among their children and grandchildren. Heirs have been shocked to learn that the tax bill on an estate can reach as much as 55 percent of the estate's total assets. To cover such an unforeseen estate tax burden, your heirs may be forced to sell the business or they may decide to keep the business going by borrowing to pay the taxes. Often, however, the debt burden prevents the heirs from investing in improvements needed for the business to remain competitive and grow.

There are solutions that can provide much relief for this burden. While your family could use other assets of the estate to pay future taxes, including life insurance, the best strategy is to plan ahead and take the steps necessary to minimize the value of the estate. To do this, you can:

- Make stock gifts to family members, thus using the annual gift tax exclusions and lifetime exemptions to transfer the current amount before the value increases;
- Gift other assets during your lifetime, thus continuing to reduce the overall estate tax; and
- Use special strategies that will allow you to leverage your gift tax exemptions, such as family partnerships, partnership freezes, grantor retained annuity trusts, and charitable trusts.

With these plans in place and a realistic assessment of your business's future tax burden, you can significantly increase the probability that the company you spent years of your life building will pass on smoothly to your heirs. By preventing unnecessary debt or a forced business sale in order to pay taxes, you can ensure that your business has the best chance to prosper.

These are just a few examples highlighting why you would want to set up a trust. However, I urge you to talk with a tax attorney who has the knowledge and experience necessary to answer your questions and lead you in the right direction.

Estate Planning

If you are still unclear on some of the issues we have discussed here, consider keeping the following list of questions to discuss with your tax attorney in further detail:

1. Would you recommend a will be prepared? Why or why not?
2. Would you recommend a trust be established? Why or why not?
3. What is probate court?
4. Why would I want to avoid probate court?
5. How can I avoid probate court?
6. What is the probate fee for my state?
7. Is establishing an estate required when someone dies?
8. How is the executor of the estate responsible for what is held in the estate?
9. Does my state have an estate tax? If so, how much is it?
10. How might the estate tax impact my heirs after my death?
11. How can my creditors take money from my estate?
12. How would a trust be funded?

When making major financial decisions that will affect your family's financial wellbeing, you need to be fully informed. Never feel embarrassed to ask questions or for further clarification on any subject that seems unclear because there are no stupid questions. Remember, people don›t plan to fail; they just fail to plan. Let's plan for success because you have worked too hard to give up everything you have worked for just because of a lack of planning.

To learn more about living trusts, watch the following video:

http://www.webprez.com/3529/69

To understand more about the importance of an estate plan, watch the following video:

http://www.webprez.com/3529/9

Chapter 5

OWNING A BUSINESS

Are you a business owner? Have you ever considered owning a business? Owning a business is a great way to build assets in your effort toward creating generational wealth because it is a way to pass something tangible to your family's next generation. It is not the only thing you can do, but it is definitely an ideal starting point.

If you have never thought about business ownership before, then now might be the time to start. If you are currently a business owner or considering becoming one, you will want to make sure that your business has been legally and properly established.

It could be said that starting a business is easy, but making sure it is correctly established is the hard part. How you establish your business is important when creating generational wealth since your goal becomes having continuous income that enables you to establish generational wealth. Seeking the guidance of a qualified and experienced attorney or Certified Public

Accountant (CPA) will give you the best opportunity to review your options and decide whether your business should be set up as a sole proprietorship, a partnership, a Limited Liability Partnership (LLP), a Limited Liability Company (LLC), an S Corporation, or a C Corporation. Depending on the type of business you establish and your goals, one designation might be preferable over the others, especially if you are considering transferring your business ownership to someone else. Again, you need to consult with a tax attorney or CPA to find out what is best for you.

Be careful about taking advice from friends or family members who care very much about your success but may not have the experience or qualifications to give advice on these matters. Additionally, do not take this matter so lightly that you decide to do it on your own. I have interviewed a lot of top tax attorneys and CPAs; they all agree that many businesses have been improperly established because people neglect to seek guidance on matters with which they are not familiar. A smart businessperson will want to establish the business properly based on the business's purpose, how the business started, who is running the business, the investments that have been made into the business, employees, income, and growth goals.

Ideally, the next question you want to think about is your exit or succession strategy; in other words, what you would like to see happen to your business should the day come that you are no longer running it? You may have never asked yourself that question. As we discussed in previous chapters, we all want to go on living forever. However, the reality is we must plan for ourselves and families before something happens and someone else plans for us. Having the proper documentation in place is always a good start, so begin with a solid estate plan as we discussed in chapter four. The key is having everything in writing so you can ensure your family gets what is rightfully theirs once you have passed.

If you pass away before you have these business affairs in order, you are unintentionally causing your family to experience multiple tragedies at once. Not only would they be grieving, but they would have the additional responsibility of cleaning up the financial mess left behind—meaning the obligation to deal with lawyers, judges, and potential trials. Just think of it this way: do not let the failure to fill out the appropriate paperwork and consult with the appropriate parties mess up the years of hard work you have put into building your business and creating a lasting legacy for your family.

Buy-Sell Agreements Through Insurance Options

For those of us who own a business and have business partners, a buy-sell agreement should be considered. You and your business partner have built this great company and both of you have a 50/50 partnership, but if there is no contract in place specifying how the money should be divided should one of you die or suffer a major illness, it can lead to a very messy legal battle. This is why you should sit down with an attorney and come to an agreement that allows both of you to put in writing how the company should be divided should one of you pass away. This document is called a buy-sell agreement. Preparing the document is one thing, but funding the document is something else.

The three ways to fund a buy-sell agreement are:

- Business bank accounts with company profits inside;
- Personal loans or business loans to buy or sell the business; and
- Life insurance (term or permanent).

For more information about how to use life insurance to fund a buy-sell agreement, view this video:

http://www.webprez.com/3529/21

Using business bank accounts is not ideal because, depending on the amount of proceeds your company has, you may need to use a majority of it just to get the agreement in place. Taking out personal or business loans is increasingly difficult because of the economic climate and banks' unwillingness to lend money as freely as they once did just a few years ago. As you can see, the first two will be the tougher and more expensive routes to take, which is why the life insurance option is the most ideal approach. Not only is it most affordable, but it simply makes the most sense.

Using life insurance to fund a buy-sell agreement is quite common in the business world, especially when it comes to using term and permanent life insurance policies. Between these two options, permanent is ideal because the amount grows with the business, creating cash value. Essentially, permanent life insurance is a whole life insurance policy with a fixed premium. A universal life insurance policy has a more flexible premium.

Term insurance is a very inexpensive policy that gives you the opportunity to purchase a large amount of life insurance for a fixed period of time, such as five, 10, 15, or 20 years. If you have an idea of how much your business will be worth in 20 years, you can purchase a large death benefit today if you believe you will die before the term is over. This is because when you purchase term insurance, you are essentially betting the insurance company that you will die before the term is reached, and the insurance company is betting that you will not.

How Whole and Universal Life Insurance Work

Let's break down whole life and universal life more specifically. Both options give you the opportunity to build cash value while enabling your policy to grow, depending on the types of options that you have inside the policy. The great thing about Whole and Universal Life Insurance is that it gives both you and your business partner the opportunity to use the cash value. In other words, if they are properly structured, the policies can grow with your business and you will not have to estimate how much your business will be worth in 20 years. You will not have to concern yourself with whether or not you will outlive the terms, as you would with term insurance.

Whole Life Insurance Compared to Universal Life Insurance

Whole Life Insurance	Universal Life Insurance
Fixed premium	Flexible premium
Fixed interest rate	Flexible interest rate
Cash value is part of the death benefit	Cash value is added to the death benefit
May pay dividends	With option B your death benefit increases
Endows at age 100	Goes beyond age 100
Cost more	Cost Less
You can take loans or do a withdrawal	You can take loans or do a withdrawal

When you set up an insurance policy and pass away, there will be enough money to be used to compensate your family for your share of the business or to compensate your business partner if your family chooses to purchase your partner's share.

A New Perspective on Life Insurance In Business

Let's say you bring in $100,000 in profits every year and when you die, your child inherits the business. Chances are your child has a great idea of how she would like to expand the company or branch out. One day, she decides to take your company from a local mom and pop shop to a nationwide business. All she needs is a million dollars to do it. Where is she going to get the money to make that idea a reality?

A bank loan would be out of the question because it is incredibly difficult to qualify for that kind of money based on credit and/or collateral. If, however, you had a life insurance policy in place before your death that was worth a million dollars or more, that money could provide the funding for your company's future growth under your child's leadership. The money could also be used to pay off Uncle Sam for any estate taxes that might be due upon your death, thus saving the business from dying with you like many businesses that are intended to be passed down. If your business was listed as the owner of your life insurance policy, the business would immediately benefit. This is called *key person life insurance.*

For more details on how key person life insurance works, access the following video:

http://www.webprez.com/3529/14

Just consider key person life insurance in this simple way: it enables businesses to put life insurance on the key person in the business. For example, say the founder and CEO of a business is the person truly behind the success of a company; this person is the reason why the business is running successfully. Should something happen to this CEO, what will happen to the business? No doubt, it will suffer. This is why a policy has to be placed on this key person to ensure there is money to keep the business afloat until you find his replacement.

Here's another example: if you had an insurance policy for yourself based on the value of your business' annual profit of $100,000, you could multiply your annual profit by ten and your company would have a policy worth $1 million. When you pass, your children or other family members will have the money available to make that million-dollar idea a reality. This type of policy should also account for any taxes that may arise. The chart below reflects options for even greater policy values to solidify your family's financial future:

Annual Profit	Multiplier	Policy Value
$100,000	10	$1,000,000
$100,000	20	$2,000,000
$100,000	30	$3,000,000
$100,000	40	$4,000,000
$100,000	50	$5,000,000

As you can see, starting a business requires more than having a clever idea that you believe may be profitable. If you are thinking of starting your own business or you already have, use the information in this chapter to get everything in order so that you have something to pass on to the next generation.

Many people start a business, but neglect to plan for the future. You should really consider getting a life insurance policy, even if you have to start with a term policy for now. You always have the option to be able to convert it at a later date when cash flow starts growing. Many people make the mistake of waiting until their business is financially successful before looking into life insurance policies. The problem with this is at that point, they might be too old and might not be able to qualify for insurance.

Note that I said "qualify" and not "afford." This is because those two are different. Some people can afford insurance, but cannot qualify for it due to illness. Some qualify, but might not be able to take advantage of overfunding the policy which makes it really beneficial to them. Still others have the cash and are able to qualify, but their advisor may not be familiar with insurance concepts and cannot properly explain the benefits life insurance holds, such as:

- *tax deferred growth*—the interest in the account grows tax free;
- *tax-free distributions*—you can access the account anytime without paying taxes as long as you take the money out in the form of a loan;
- *collateral opportunities*—you can use the cash value as collateral to get loans;
- *liquidity of funds*—no penalties or restrictions when you need to take your money out;
- *no-loss provisions*—you can never lose your money based on stock market fluctuations;
- *guaranteed loan options*—you are always guaranteed a loan against your cash value without any credit checks;
- *safe harbor*—your cash value is always safe from creditors and everyone else who tries to come after your cash;
- *no limits on contributions*—you can put in as much money as you want based on the size of your policy and your age up to the maximum allowed by the IRS;

- *no age restrictions*—regardless of your age, you can purchase life insurance up to age 85 (with some companies and some up to age 90) and is a good way to leave TAX free money to your loved ones; and
- *deductible opportunities for business owners, if properly structured*—if properly structured, you can actually deduct some of your life insurance premiums, just like you do with an IRA, and still access the cash tax free without any IRS penalty and/or taxes.

Chapter 6

OWNING REAL ESTATE

I cannot reiterate this enough: when a family member dies, it's stressful. So many people find themselves ill-prepared because they failed to have the crucial conversations before tragedy struck. Obviously, no one wants to talk about what should be done when a family member passes, but talking about and planning for it will save you from a lot of trouble down the road.

One of the more important conversations you need to have is what will happen to your home once you and your partner pass away. Will your children take over or will they sell it? The family home is a very big deal and not just for sentimental reasons. For many Americans, their home is their biggest investment. It's the most expensive thing they own and deciding to purchase it was one of their biggest life decisions. So why not make sure that it is properly handled?

Many parents fail to have this discussion with their children. Instead, they assume and trust that their children will know just what to do with the house when something happens to them. Ask yourself these questions:

1. Will your children truly know what to do with your house when you pass?
2. Do they know what you would like them to do?
3. Will they understand how to care for the property you worked so hard to own?
4. Will they be prepared for the additional costs of keeping or selling your home?
5. Will they know the power of the equity you have built up over the years?

When speaking to your children, those are the questions you should answer for them. We have already talked a great deal about the documents you should have in place: a living trust, life insurance, etc. It is important to understand that all of these elements must come together to protect your home, your business, your finances and, in a broader sense, to help create generational wealth. It's my goal to drill this into your head: you *must* have the proper documents in place.

Should you pass, your children should know that they must immediately call the family attorney to ensure that all the documents are lined up properly. And do not forget to make your children aware of where you are keeping all of your important documents. It's no use doing the work to have the proper documents in order if your children can't access them when they need them the most! I recommend putting all of the documents in one place, preferably a secure safe, bank safety deposit box or another secured but accessible location. Also, make sure your attorney has copies of all these documents.

Should your children sell your home after you pass? There is no right answer to that question. Take me, for example. My documents ensure that my homes, land, and any stock I acquire will not be sold for a certain time period after I pass. I prefer to maintain my homes and land as assets in our family trust and allow the property values to grow until they reach a certain amount. As a parent, it is up to you to decide how you want your home to be handled and ensure that the proper documentation is put into place so that your wishes are fulfilled.

Obviously, many things can happen between here and death. Will your children have to sell your home to get the money to care for you because you do not have long-term care insurance? If you need to go to a nursing home, but do not have enough savings, the federal government will come to your assistance with Medicare. The process requires that the government place a lien on your home that your children will have to pay. Having real estate puts you in a position of power because you have an asset that can work for you financially. The question becomes, however, what can you do now to ensure that if that time comes the process can go as smoothly as possible? Is your family aware of how the process works? These are just some of the many issues you need to discuss extensively. Ideally, these conversations should be had before disaster strikes.

Acquiring land and rental properties is also a big deal and clearly something you will have to take into account when making arrangements. Congratulations if you have had the courage and financial ability to make these investments, but I must ask you: how have you handled recording ownership? Did you know that if you have to go to a nursing home, your assets must be declared to determine if you financially qualify to receive necessary healthcare? Part of the qualification process will include you selling off every one of your properties and taking that money to pay for your care. If your wealth is not protected properly, you can lose all of the real estate investments you have spent your life working to acquire.

Yet again, this is why estate planning is such an important aspect of protecting yourself financially. Please consult with a board certified estate attorney to determine the best way to manage your real estate.

Chapter 7

YOUR WEALTH LEGACY

Now is the time to introduce you to the private reserve account I have mentioned over and over again.

Questions number five, six, and seven on our list are:

6. Do you have children?
7. Do you own a private reserve account for you and your spouse?
8. Do you have a private reserve account for each of your children?

All of these questions relate to life insurance. We will soon learn that life insurance policies are your best option for creating generational wealth, no matter what your current income level or the amount of assets you currently have.

The history of life insurance goes back to the ancient Romans. There is a reason it continues to be a highly utilized tool in our financial arsenals: it is the only vehicle in America where there are no taxes. In essence, you are using pennies to buy dollars, and life insurance policies are powerful tools in creating generational wealth.

There are a couple of reasons why many people find it useless or even in poor taste to take out a life insurance policy on a child. The first is they believe it is betting on the child dying, but that is false. The second misconception is that it is useless because they do not have assets. Life insurance policies are not about children having assets. With a child in particular, you are actually betting on the fact that they are going to have a long life and be around for many more years. Not only is it cheaper to buy a policy for a child, but if you take out a $1 million universal life or index universal life insurance policy on your child, by the time he or she is old enough to benefit from the money, it will be worth millions of dollars more. This is money that can be used to create generational wealth.

Many fail to realize that life insurance policies are very valuable to the living, not just valuable to the family of the deceased. This is because the money paid into a life insurance policy can be borrowed against, which is especially useful during retirement because the money can be used without having to pay taxes to the IRS.

Personally, I have greatly benefited from borrowing against the money paid into my life insurance policy. For example, rather than using my savings to pay for our beautiful wedding or when helping my wife open her clinic, I utilized my life insurance account. The same could be done for your children. Remember when 2012 presidential hopeful Mitt Romney infamously told a young student to "borrow money" from his parents to start a business? Well, what happens if you are like most American children whose parents do not have the money to give for a business? In order to be an entrepreneur or take advantage of investment opportunities, you have to have money to begin with—not a great deal, but enough to get the ball rolling on a new endeavor. The answer, if you have been following, is clearly borrowing against your policy! If you take out a policy when your child is born, by the time they are in their 20s, they can borrow against the account and utilize the funds to pay off their college loans, start a new business, or enter graduate school. Most people will argue and question why they should borrow from their life insurance policy. Well, one reason is that the interest rate is lower than most banks. Secondly, you do not have to qualify to secure the loan. Finally, you are borrowing from and repaying yourself.

Utilizing life insurance for more than death benefits is not a new concept. Surely, we've all heard of the popular chain of department stores called J.C. Penney. Back in 1898, James Cash Penney, Jr. began working for a small chain of stores. In 1902, the owners offered him one-third partnership in a new store he would open. After investing just $2,000 in what would eventually become a multi-billion dollar chain, Penney opened his first store in Wyoming, and soon enough, he opened another. Shortly after, the original owners dissolved their partnership and Penney purchased full interest in all existing stores. By 1913, Penney had dozens of stores and had incorporated the company (another thing we have learned about) under the new name, J. C. Penney Company.

The Great Depression and the stock market crash of 1929 left Penney virtually penniless, but he was able to borrow against his life insurance policies to help the company meet its payroll—a strategy that would save the company, which still exists today.

As you can see, life insurance benefits the living and can be a major step in creating generational wealth. There are different types of life insurance policies. The key to finding the right one is sitting down with a great financial advisor who understands your financial needs and understands how you plan to eventually utilize your life insurance policy. Again, this book is like your travel companion for creating generational wealth, but that does not mean you do not need to consult with advisors and other professionals along the way.

This book is really about thinking outside of the box. These days, banks will make you jump through tons of hoops for the smallest loan, but as we have discussed, there are other ways to help your children and create generational wealth. Essentially, if you have a life insurance policy, it means you have other options available to you so you do not have to rely on fickle banks to make your family's dreams a possibility. Knowledge is power, which is another reason why what we are discussing can change the course of your family's financial future. Pass this information to your children, your friends, and your family members. Help everyone you know and love learn about the benefits of life insurance policies so that they, too, can forge their own financial paths.

When it comes to financial planning, the idea of including a chapter on children might seem a little unusual, but when you are discussing creating generational wealth, it makes all the sense in the world.

The main reason most parents work so hard is to make sure their children have all the things they need and want in life, within reason. We want to provide a roof over their heads, good food on the table, nice clothing to wear, and a competitive education. As parents, it is not our goal that our children will follow our footsteps, but that they will be able to go above and beyond us and achieve more than we dared dream to and improve each generation.

What many parents fail to do is insure their children's lives. Many think it is morbid. Many have been advised not to because children do not earn income, so they equate this type of insurance policy with debt. There are actually countless benefits. Not only is a policy inexpensive, but the child does not have to undergo a medical exam, and it makes more sense than opening up a savings account, which earns interest very slowly. The cash value of a policy increases as the policy earns interest. There are some rules regarding children's life insurance policies that you should be mindful of. For example, your child cannot have more life insurance than you. Meaning, you can't have a million dollar policy on your child when you only have a $100,000 policy.

One of my clients has a young daughter. He decided to place $1 million life insurance policy on her as a way of investing in her future. Again, the goal is to create generational wealth. Each month, he pays $500 into his daughter's policy. The actual premium is only $100 dollars, but he is overfunding it up to the Modified Endowment Contract (MEC) limit, the maximum amount allowed by the IRS. When she turns 25, the policy cash value could be up to $250,000. The family trust owns the policy. That is not just life changing money, but money that can change a family for generations to come. It is my client's hope that his daughter lives a long and prosperous life. When she eventually passes, that invested money will go into a trust. For instance, if she were to live beyond age 75, the life insurance policy he places on her as an infant will be worth several million dollars. The cycle will be repeated again and again from one generation to the next generation. Note, cash value growth may not be guaranteed; however, the base value of the policy will never decrease.

When we fail to plan properly, our kids may end up being worse off than us, or in some cases, they may continue to perpetuate a cycle of poverty. Perhaps it is our fault because we did not have the education, the motivation, or the information needed to make intelligent financial decisions. Or, it could simply be a case of our children not appreciating the work we have put into acquiring the wealth we have, so they blow through the money once they receive their inheritance or trust fund—if they are lucky enough to have one.

Educating Your Children About Finances

I understand that not everyone can afford to pay $500 a month for a child's life insurance policy. I also understand that many families these days are operating without any extra income, making purchasing a policy out of the question. It is important for you to understand that information is just as valuable as money, sometimes even more so. You may not have the funds to set up your family the way you would like, but you can pass this information onto your family, instill it in your children, and make sure they take these steps. Knowledge is power or, in this case, applied knowledge is power. Knowledge can shape your family's financial future.

You have to ensure that you are not raising careless children who make bad decisions. If your family becomes well off and one of your children marries someone you feel isn't right for them, make sure a prenuptial agreement is signed. If your teenager wants an expensive car that you can afford to give them, make sure they are driving responsibly because if an accident occurs, any victims in the car could sue your family for retribution, leaving you swimming in legal bills and debt. As you can see, it is not just about raising your kids to be smart about money; it's about raising your kids to be smart, period.

It seems that many Americans operate with the understanding that they should not discuss finances with their children. It is almost taboo, with the belief being that talking about money will be unnecessarily stressful for their children or that they are too young to worry about such things. I believe that approach is part of the problem. It is part of the reason why so many children today do not value what they are given or have a true understanding of money. The federal government mandates a nationwide minimum wage level of $7.25 per hour, yet children expect to have iPads like their classmates, not understanding that the $500 gadget is almost a week and a half's pay.

As my daughter gets older, I will talk to her extensively about finances and what it means to be fiscally responsible. She will understand the value of a dollar because we will discuss these things regularly at the dinner table.

I like to use this analogy:

Your family is a business. One parent is the president, the other is the vice president, and the children are employees. A family has income and expenses like a business, right? How are you going to successfully maintain this business? In this respect, it makes a great deal of sense to talk to your children—or employees—about how they contribute to the bigger picture, about how you are all working toward this common goal.

College Funding for Children

Funding is another major issue for families who want their children to attend college but are not aware of how expensive their college of choice will be in the future. By the time a child is ready to go to college, the parents are faced with the dilemma of not having enough money to pay for their education. The parents feel guilty and begin taking money out of their retirement accounts, home equity, and personal saving accounts. They get second jobs just because they feel badly about not being able to fund their children's education. I tell my clients to deal with first things first. Let's determine how much it will likely cost to attend college. If you do not know what it will cost, how can you plan for it?

Some parents open a savings account for their children because they want to teach them the importance of saving money for their future. They also designate this money as a college fund with hopes that it will be enough. Some even go as far as setting up a 529 college plan for the child as well. When I ask how much they are contributing, they are often saving $50 or $100 monthly in a 529 college plan. When I ask what college they want their child to attend, their answer is not specific. They are often unclear about projected college costs in 18 years and surprised that these costs increase annually by an average of 6%.

I encourage my clients to apply for financial aid first because it is free money. They are often surprised to find out how much they qualify for. Many parents believe their children might not qualify for financial aid because they make too much money. In all of my years of working with parents and doing research, I have found that income is just one part of the financial aid qualification process. There are other factors. Do not eliminate yourself from the consideration pool just because you think you will not qualify.

Scholarships are another option. What do you do if your child does not qualify for any scholarships? Will you tell them to not consider college at all? Will you abandon them and leave them to fend for themselves? Of course not! We still love them regardless. Yes, as "employees," they were provided with everything needed to be successful in school; however, our children will not always do their part to perform at their highest potential to obtain the scholarships. Realistically, not all children CAN perform at that level. In a desire to do whatever we can to support their success (or our guilt), we start depleting our assets and using our savings and retirement funds to send our kids to college because we do not want them to obtain student loans.

So what do you do? For many parents, just the idea of their child having to take out a student loan leaves a bad taste in their mouths. This is mostly because once the child graduates, parents want them to start with a clean slate, but with student loan debt, that's hardly what they get upon completing their studies, or so it's assumed.

If my children do not qualify for financial aid or obtain scholarships, I have a plan B. My children will secure student loans but not just *any* student loan—the right student loan. There are government-subsidized student loans with better rates than other loan options. Some loans will enable your child to pay off the debt by doing volunteer work in another country.

For example, have your child look into the Federal Perkins Loan, otherwise known as a Perkins Loan. This student loan carries a fixed interest rate of five percent for the duration of its 10-year repayment period. The low interest rate comes as a result of the loan being granted by the U.S. Department of Education. This loan has a nine-month grace period, meaning borrowers do not have to begin repayment until ten months after they have graduated. Another benefit of obtaining a loan

Your Wealth Legacy

subsidized by the government is that interest does not begin to accrue until the borrower begins to repay the loan. There are loan limits, however. For undergraduates, it's $5,500 with a lifetime maximum loan of $27,500. It is a bit more for graduate students, with the limit being $8,000 per year, with a lifetime limit of $60,000.

If your child is interested in repaying a portion of their loan by doing volunteer work, there are programs oriented towards specific careers, such as teaching or nursing. For example, if your child enters the healthcare field, there are programs supported by the government that forgive student loans if he or she works for a federally qualified health clinic. Others are open to recent graduates who meet certain income and eligibility requirements, but some exist that will take just about anyone.

Take SponsorChange.org, for example. This non-profit organization provides a way for people to donate directly to skills-based service projects, which are completed by college graduates in exchange for student loan pay. The most well known volunteer option is AmeriCorps, a national network of service programs that requires students to volunteer for a year full-time. In exchange, they get a small living stipend. When the year is up, an education award of $4,725 can be applied to student loan debt. This money can also be applied to future educational endeavors, depending on where your child is in their educational pursuits.

Lastly, there is always the Peace Corps, which requires volunteers to make a two-year commitment to serve in a foreign country. Unlike AmeriCorps, the Peace Corps does *not* provide a student loan payment award, but it allows participants with federal loan programs to defer their loan payments while serving in the Peace Corps. According to the Peace Corps website, those with federal Perkins Loans are eligible for a partial cancellation benefit of 15 percent for one year of service and up to 70 percent for four years. The program also provides participants with a $6,000 readjustment allowance after the two-year term of service is completed, a portion of which can be used to repay student loan debt.

Many people are under the impression that student loans are always bad, but there are good loans and bad loans; it's all in how you use them. We have all heard before that there is good debt and bad debt. Well, the same logic applies to student loans. Having a mortgage is a good debt. Taking out a small business loan is good debt, and a college loan is good debt as well because you are using the money to improve your life and increase your earnings potential. Let's not be so hard on ourselves! If your child has to take out a student loan, it's not a horrible thing, especially with some of the options we have just outlined. President Obama recently paid off his student loans, and he will be the first to tell you that acquiring debt in order to obtain an education is definitely worth it.

The key to having a student loan is having a plan B. What is that plan B? Let me share an example.

My wife comes from a family of four children. Not only did her two older siblings go to college and obtain doctoral degrees, but my wife was able to graduate with a Master's degree at the age of 23. When she graduated, she had student loan debt equaling $80,000, but that did not stop her from purchasing a home and maintaining a credit score of 800 plus. You see, student loan debt is not the end of your life. It may feel overwhelming at times, but if you have "good" debt, you are going to be okay—just like my wife, whose degree was able to secure her a well-paying job. She still continues paying her student loan and is able to deduct the interest for income tax purposes.

Surely, it's the dream of all parents to simply write a check and pay for their child's entire college education, or write a check that can wipe away all of their debt. What many do not know is that there is a way for you to relieve your children of a great deal of their financial burden. You can actually use a life insurance policy's cash value to offset and pay off your child's student loan.

This is why it's crucial for you to start a small cash value life insurance policy for your children, which is your plan B. It gives them a good head start in life. Keep in mind that I am not suggesting that money be used to fund their entire education when they turn 18, but that money can be used to help pay off their college loans or to assist them in starting their first business upon graduating from college. It can also help them purchase their first home or their first car, fund a wedding, or whatever the money is needed for. Also, keep in mind that you are in full control of the money—not your kids—so this will ensure that you can keep the money safe until they're old enough to make wise decisions about how they will use it. The younger your child is when you start his or her insurance policy, the better off they will be in the long run.

Chances are you have been cautioned against taking out a life insurance policy on your child, but I firmly believe it can be a good thing. Just think of it from your child's perspective. Say she is now 35-years-old. How different could her life be if you had started saving money for her in an account that grew tax-deferred and could be accessed tax-free? Just $100 a month from the time your child is born until the day she turns 35 would give her immediate access to at least $100,000 tax-free using an average of a 5% rate of return compounding over 35 years. That money can be designated to maybe start a business, help pay off any student loans, or whatever the child chooses to use the money for that would benefit her. That is the kind of money that could make a major difference in a person's life, and you can give that gift to your child if you plan ahead. Remember, folks: this is not a new concept; it has been around for centuries and the wealthy have always used life insurance to create massive amounts of wealth for future generations. Now you can, too.

To understand more about college funding options, watch the following video:

http://www.webprez.com/3529/44

Chapter 8

LIFE INSURANCE: THE KEY TO BUILDING YOUR FAMILY WEALTH LEGACY

Countless people spend hundreds of dollars on Lotto tickets every year even though their chances of winning are one in 20 million. These same people do not see the need to purchase life insurance, which will guarantee 100% of the family's money should the person pass away. If we know anything in life, it's that we will one day die, so why not bet on a sure thing rather than throwing your money at an unrealistic dream? I have never understood this. Those are guaranteed odds, but so few people take advantage!

The wealthy understand these odds. They invest heavily in life insurance and use life insurance as a way to build and create generational wealth. If you have ever wondered why the poor stay poor and the wealthy stay wealthy, that's one of the reasons.

The following video will provide more insight regarding how to establish your own private bank:

http://www.webprez.com/3529/37

Consider, for example, that when you apply for a business or residential loan, one of the key assets that a bank will ask you to disclose is life insurance. Snapshots from actual loan applications below reflect that requirement. Similarly, if you evaluate the assets in which most financial institutions invest, life insurance will be a part of that portfolio. The third image reflects the insurance assets for all commercial banks insured by the FDIC (lines 42-45).

RESIDENTIAL LOAN APPLICATION

Acct. no.	$	Acct. no.
Stocks & Bonds (Company name/ number & description)	$	Name and address of C
		Acct. no.
Life insurance net cash value	$	Name and address of C
Face amount: $		
Subtotal Liquid Assets	$ 0.00	
Real estate owned (enter market value from schedule of real estate owned)	$	
Vested interest in retirement fund	$	

BUSINESS LOAN APPLICATION

Business Name of Applicant/Borrower

ASSETS		(Omit Cents)	
Cash on hand & in Banks	$		Accounts
Savings Accounts	$		Notes Pay
IRA or Other Retirement Account	$		(Desc
Accounts & Notes Receivable	$		Installmen
Life Insurance-Cash Surrender Value Only (Complete Section 8)	$		Mo. P
			Installmen
Stocks and Bonds (Describe in Section 3)	$		Mo. P
			Loan on L
Real Estate (Describe in Section 4)	$		Mortgages
			(Desc
Automobile-Present Value	$		Unpaid Ta
Other Personal Property	$		(Desc

FDIC - Statistics on Depository Institutions Report

Note: Go to the end to obtain a key report for the column selections. Go to Key

Assets and Liabilities
Report Menu: (Tiered) [Update Report]

Report Date: 6/30/2013
Data Type: Dollars
Income Basis: Year-to-Date
Data Format: Total (Sum)

	All Commercial Banks - National 6/30/2013 $ in 000's Total (Sum)	All Commercial Banks - Assets less than $100M National 6/30/2013 $ in 000's Total (Sum)	All Commercial Banks - Assets $100M to $1B - National 6/30/2013 $ in 000's Total (Sum)	All Commercial Banks - Assets more than $1B - National 6/30/2013 $ in 000's Total (Sum)
26 **Total equity capital**	1,500,553,624	12,651,970	111,488,708	1,376,412,946
27 Total bank equity capital	1,485,758,971	12,650,633	111,422,433	1,361,685,905
28 Perpetual preferred stock	4,570,547	59,536	994,398	3,516,613
29 Common stock	42,975,322	1,577,211	10,997,312	30,400,799
30 Surplus	1,057,710,771	6,082,066	51,996,316	999,632,389
31 Undivided profits	380,502,330	4,931,820	47,434,407	328,136,103
32 Noncontrolling interests in consolidated subsidiaries	14,794,653	1,337	66,275	14,727,041
Memoranda:				
33 Noncurrent loans and leases	220,973,392	1,206,921	13,774,186	205,992,286
34 Noncurrent loans that are wholly or partially guaranteed by the U.S. government	72,855,995	48,574	500,466	72,306,955
35 Income earned, not collected on loans	39,560,957	650,748	4,477,622	34,432,587
36 Earning assets	11,723,975,962	101,549,657	966,885,509	10,655,540,796
37 Long-term assets (5+ years)	3,194,859,465	29,847,619	307,582,559	2,857,429,287
38 Average Assets, year-to-date	13,351,146,626	112,271,242	1,053,130,124	12,185,745,259
39 Average Assets, quarterly	13,345,433,029	112,481,727	1,052,730,626	12,180,220,677
40 Total risk weighted assets	9,365,632,217	68,381,206	708,585,416	8,588,665,595
41 Adjusted average assets for leverage capital purposes	12,869,848,368	112,077,628	1,044,609,050	11,713,161,690
42 (Life insurance assets)	131,204,014	809,809	10,987,210	119,406,995
43 General account life insurance assets	51,071,330	676,620	8,531,831	41,862,879
44 Separate account life insurance assets	67,587,766	53,644	726,895	66,807,227
45 Hybrid life insurance assets	12,544,918	79,545	1,728,484	10,736,899
46 Volatile liabilities	2,645,262,505	5,245,244	71,323,891	2,568,693,370

Can you see how important life insurance is as a wealth building asset? If it is that valuable to the largest financial institutions in the world, shouldn't it be part of your financial portfolio? As we've already learned, life insurance policies have so many uses for the living, but clearly they would also be incredibly useful when someone passes. It's not just smart to have a life insurance policy; it is responsible, so as not to burden your family with all the costs resulting from the funeral. With the average cost of an American funeral averaging $10,000, a life insurance policy becomes all the more important. You see, the wealthy understand that death will come so they plan for it using the tax-free law of the land to their advantage.

I often think, "What if my dad was savvy enough to have started a million dollar life insurance policy for himself years ago? How much would that policy have been worth when he passed away at age 76?" What a life-changing difference the policy would have made, not only for me, but for my mother (who now lives with me), my siblings, and all of the grandchildren. I often wonder how the lives of my brothers back in Nigeria could have been impacted had they each been given a check for $100,000 from my father's life insurance policy. In Africa, $1 goes a long way. Just think of how different their lives might have been if my father planned properly.

For every major breadwinner in a family, there should be a life insurance policy in place for ten times the income amount they currently make. For example, if I am earning $100,000 each year, there needs to be a $1 million life insurance policy on me so if I should die, my wife has enough money to keep our family afloat until she figures out what to do next.

By this point, you have heard me use the word "wealthy" quite a bit. You need to understand there is a difference between the wealthy and the rich.

When I entered the financial services industry and began to do my own research on generational wealth, that's when I discovered the secrets behind the truly wealthy. One of the secrets is something we have already discussed: cash value life insurance policies. Another secret is family trusts, which ensure that any family wealth that is acquired will be passed on to the next generation estate tax-free. Even if the family has to pay taxes, they will pay very little in comparison to those who do not have a family trust.

I understand that some of the concepts I've introduced may be difficult to conceive, but my intention is to expand your knowledge about personal financial options that you may not have been previously aware of. Beyond just having this knowledge, applying it to real life is what counts. I have the personal experience of implementing this unique financial strategy of using life insurance as my own "bank" in many instances in my life. It may sound bizarre, but I have paid off cars with life insurance. I financed my wedding with life insurance. As I mentioned previously, I even helped my wife open her own medical clinic with life insurance.

These are the successes, but I made one mistake many years ago without fully knowing my options. My Dad was sick, and I needed to send him to India for medical treatment. The total expense was approximately $30,000. I withdrew the money from my SEP IRA and thought I had 60 business days to return the money to the account. However, the IRS allowed 60 calendar days to return the money to the account. That error cost me $11,400 in taxes and penalties. Many of you will consider withdrawing money from your retirement accounts to fund your needs and dreams. This is why I want to show you another option and teach you different ways to manage your finances. I hope to pass on knowledge even more than generational wealth is.

Chapter 9

CREATING GENERATIONAL WEALTH WITH THE RIGHT POLICIES

The life insurance death benefit is the only investment vehicle in the U.S. that is not taxed when properly structured. Lottery winners pay taxes on their winnings, people pay taxes on real estate investments, on stocks, and on businesses, but if a life insurance policy is properly structured and owned, its beneficiaries do not pay taxes on the death benefit proceeds. This is something the wealthy have always understood, which is why they purchase many life insurance policies, all of which are tied to the family trust.

In chapter six, we discussed how running your family like a business can help family members understand how everyone contributes to the family's success and financial wellbeing. Further illustrating that point, it is important for you to understand that banks and major corporations use life insurance as part of their assets.

Bank-Owned Life Insurance (BOLI) is a form of life insurance purchased by banks where the bank is the beneficiary and/or owner. This form of insurance is a tax shelter for the administering bank. Banks use BOLI contracts to fund ever-increasing employee benefits at a much cheaper rate. The process works like this: the bank sets up the contract and then makes payments into a specialized fund operating as the insurance trust. All employee benefits covered under the plan are paid out from this fund.

For corporations, this is called COLI (Corporation-Owned Life Insurance). The most notable benefit of implementing COLI is after-tax net income. This benefit arises when the cash value of the policy becomes larger than the premiums paid. Based on 2009 industry surveys completed by Clark Consulting, 71 percent of Fortune 1000 companies finance Supplemental Executive Retirement Plan (SERP) obligations with COLI programs. Also, of the top 50 banks in the United States, 43 have implemented COLI programs.

Some of you must be scratching your heads, thinking, "What does any of this have to do with me?" You are right! Unless you own a bank or major corporation, BOLI and COLI do not apply to you, but this is information worth pointing out. What you should take away from this is the understanding that major corporations and financial institutions have been utilizing life insurance for decades now, so why not take a cue from the best? Why not utilize what those in the know have been banking their success on—quite literally—for years now? We could all stand to learn something from corporations who have remained successful during the recession, countless economic downturns, acquisitions, and all kinds of other challenges. The major take away from these corporate practices is utilizing life insurance can be a game changer for you and your family.

Using Life Insurance as a Financial Strategy

As promised, I want to share with you how life insurance policies have personally benefited me. When I purchased my life insurance policy before I started my family, I used the policy as my own private savings account. Rather than putting money in a traditional savings account, which accrues very little interest each year, I purchased an index universal life insurance policy and use that as my own private savings account. I only have a checking account at a bank to pay my bills like everyone else. When I need large sums of money, as I did for my wedding or when my wife wanted to open up a medical clinic, I utilize my life insurance funds. Not only do life insurance policies have a better interest rate than traditional savings accounts (a whopping six percent, compared to an average of 0.3% for savings accounts), but life insurance policies are also more secure and grow tax-deferred. No penalties are associated with loans or withdrawals, and the money inside the policy is accessible to you at any time, no questions asked. What could be better than that?

Eventually, I was able to use the money from my cash value policy to purchase mutual funds and stocks for more aggressive returns. I also purchased real estate. Obviously, this did not happen overnight; however, as my business income grew, I invested more and put more money into my life insurance policy.

The goal was to continue setting my family up for generational wealth and leave behind a legacy.

Life insurance is very inexpensive for children and, as scientists have confirmed, humans will live longer than ever before as the medical field continues to advance. So, it is not out of the question to assume that your children will easily live into their 90s, meaning a life insurance policy could eventually be worth hundreds of millions of dollars. You see the wealthy put life insurance on their children because they are betting they will live long, productive lives. Thus, they buy large amounts of coverage on their children. The insurance rule is your children cannot have more life insurance than what you personally have. For example, you cannot have $100,000 policy on yourself and put $1,000,000 in coverage on your child. However, if you have a $2,000,000 policy on yourself, you can put $1,000,000 on your child. Each child should be equally insured. Basically, you can cover your children for up to half of the amount of the policy that you have for yourself.

With that said, the children of wealthy parents have more coverage on them because their parents started their plans a long time ago, which allows the cycle to continue for generations. This money will be handed to the next generation tax-free, changing the course of their futures forever. This is also why it is important to set up the family trust early, making sure to name the trust as the owner and beneficiary of the life insurance policy. Funding the family trust will expand the family's wealth because the money can be used to purchase a business, rental properties, land, and essentially generate more income for the family trust. The life insurance becomes the source of liquid cash that is infused into the trust when any of the family members pass away.

These options have been around for years, and wealthy families have utilized them for generations. So many American dynasties have utilized cash value life insurance to expand their wealth and pass it down from one generation to the next. It is important to note that cash value life insurance policies are not the only type that can be utilized as a personal savings account, but they are the most preferable. Here's why:

- The interest is tax-deferred;
- The cash value can also be distributed tax-free (if you cancel the policy, taxes may be due);
- You can make high contributions into the policy;
- You can use the policy as collateral;
- There are guaranteed loan options without credit checks;
- When paying back any amount that has been borrowed, you get to choose the amount. The payment amount is not dictated by the company, and your payments are unstructured, which means you control your payback option;
- You get competitive returns;
- These policies provide life-long protection;
- Because these policies do not need to be renewed, declining health will not affect your insurability unless you want to purchase more insurance;
- You may borrow against your cash value funds at any time and for any reason; and
- You have liquidity.

Understanding Term Life Insurance

Life insurance is even probate-free if there is a named beneficiary. So, why don't so-called-experts talk about any of this? Because they would rather focus on term life insurance, which I do provide, but I use it in a way that gives my clients the opportunity to get the maximum amount of coverage for a temporary amount of time like 5, 10, 15, 20, or 30 years. My clients can qualify for term life insurance until they can convert it to cash value life insurance at a later date, but we always sell them a small cash value life policy on the side to grow with the term.

Let's say I have a 30-year-old client who makes $50,000-a-year and wants a million dollar permanent life insurance policy. The problem is that a $1 million cash value life insurance policy will cost $700 a month and chances are the client can't afford an extra $700 monthly expenditure on top of their other responsibilities.

What I advise is that the client obtains a cash value policy and a term life insurance policy. Here's why:

Paying $700 a month into a cash value life insurance policy might be out of the question, but $300 a month is much easier on the wallet and much more doable for someone making $50,000 a year. The client can opt for a 30-year standalone term life insurance policy for $900,000, with the premium being around $136. At the same time, he will purchase a $100,000 index universal life insurance policy that builds cash value, which will cost him approximately $68. He will put the remaining $96 into his index universal life insurance policy so he can build more cash value. This helps him meet his $1,000,000 coverage need within his $300 budget. This is one of the many reasons I love using universal life insurance policies when working with clients under age 55. Combined, they will be paying a total of $300 a month, which is clearly more reasonable than $700 a month.

Five to 10 years from now when the client is able to afford making a monthly payment of $700, the $900,000 term life insurance policy can be converted into the $100,000 cash value policy, turning it into a $1 million cash value policy. Why is this ideal? You do not have to purchase a new policy, making the most of the money the client has already been investing for the past 10 years. Also, the older you get, the more policies cost because companies take your age and health into account, often requiring an exam before a policy can be purchased. Because the client purchased the policy at the age of 30 and is choosing to convert the policy rather than purchase a new one, a health exam is not required, and he also was able to lock in at his previously quoted rate of $700 by increasing his $100,000 permanent life to a million dollar policy at a later time.

To simplify the idea, think of it like this: you want a beautiful house, but you can't afford to pay for it outright. So, you begin by purchasing one room. The following year, you purchase another room. The year after that, you purchase the third room. Before long, you have taken over every room, so the house is yours. That is the essential idea behind combining a term life insurance policy with a cash value life insurance policy, enabling the small cash value policy to grow with the term. You settle for two smaller policies, paying what you can, until you can afford the $1 million policy.

It goes without saying that to truly make this approach work for you, you need to consult a professional insurance agent who understands how cash value life insurance works; the best way to make sure you are speaking to the right person is to request that the agent share his or her policy with you. Your agent must also understand how term life insurance works and should have access to multiple companies and products including term, whole life, and universal life policies. They should be able to explain how they have used their policy or why this approach is something they would personally recommend. Why is this important? It's absolutely necessary that you are working with someone who practices what he or she preaches.

Personally, I have never had a problem sharing with my clients. I outline the policies I have, why they work for me, what I have been able to do as a result of having these policies. Most importantly, I also share what did not work for me. It seems that many clients are apprehensive to ask their agents what kind of policies they have and why, thinking those questions are too personal. They are not! Your agent should be able to show you by example; if your agent has a problem with you asking these questions, then that should be a red flag. Essentially, you want to know what they are recommending to you is good enough for them. If it's not, perhaps it is time to find another agent or call me J!

I understand that throughout the course of this book, you might feel overwhelmed, inundated by new information, and concerned that it's too late to set something in motion for yourself. Please believe me when I say that is simply not true. The example in this chapter featuring the 30-year-old making $50,000 is just an example. Do not feel dejected because you are well over 30 or making much less than a $50,000 salary. Chances are many of you are starting from scratch. Frankly, you may not experience wealth or financial comfort over the course of your lifetime, but that is no reason to give up hope. Everyone reading these words has the power to change the course of their family's financial future. Right now, you can take the steps necessary to ensure that your loved ones are not only taken care of when you pass, but given opportunities you only dreamed of. No matter what your age or income, it is never too late to set the stage for creating generational wealth, and it starts right now with you.

Chapter 10

DAVID'S STORY

Utilizing the Tax Law to His Advantage

Admittedly, this is my favorite chapter because I get to teach you about the rules of the money game. To illustrate these rules, I would like to tell you about a young man named David who came to one of my financial seminars after relocating to Tampa, Florida. David's story helps me illustrate a very important concept: *Taxes Now, Taxes Later, and Taxes Never*. Understanding this concept is the difference between knowing how to use tax law in your favor and how tax law may work against you.

Taxes Now

As we discussed previously, the IRS is always thinking of ways to ensure they get a piece of the pie—the "pie" being your finances. It is possible, however, to play by the rules *and* save a large percentage of your money from taxes.

When I say "Taxes Now," it means the earnings generated from certain investment vehicles will be taxed each year. The investment vehicles that fall under taxes now include savings accounts, certificates of deposit (CDs), money market accounts, mutual funds, stocks, and real estate. The advantages of these investment vehicles are:

- No age limit;
- No IRS withdrawal restrictions (when you want to withdraw the money, these funds are liquid);
- No limit to how much you can invest; and
- Withdrawal without IRS penalty or taxation.

You will, however, pay taxes on the following:

- interest earned from savings, CDs, and money market accounts;
- capital gains and dividends generated by stocks and mutual funds; and
- earnings from real estate.

All of these accounts are subject to probate, creditor attachments, lawsuits, and liens. Every year, you will have to report these earnings to the IRS when you file your taxes, which means the IRS will tax you for these earnings—hence "Taxes Now."

If you are involved in an automobile accident and an injured party sues you for an amount exceeding your automobile insurance coverage, you may be taken to court and have a lien placed on any of these investment vehicles to satisfy a judgment. Later in this chapter, I will share other investment vehicles that enable you to receive the same benefits and provide protection against the disadvantages outlined for the options listed above.

David's Story

The last situation you want is to work hard and place your earnings in an unprotected account.

The Federal Deposit Insurance Corporation (FDIC) protects funds in deposit accounts up to $250,000 per depositor in case the bank files for bankruptcy or goes out of business like we experienced in 2008. You can find a list of these failed banks on the FDIC website. If you have $500,000 in a single account, the FDIC will only protect $250,000. Your funds are not protected from creditor attachments, lawsuits, and liens.

Let me paint the picture for you: these "taxes now" investment vehicles are like parking your car on the street. If you do not pay your car payment and the repossession company wants to take your car, they can. It is easy to find. These accounts operate the same way if someone wants to stake a claim against your "taxes now" investment vehicles.

Let's get back to David, who is a 30-year-old guy making $50,000 a year. His job does not offer a retirement plan, so he decides to save in one of the "Taxes Now" accounts mentioned previously. David did not consult with an advisor, so he thinks this will be the best route.

After taxes, David takes home $37,500 a year, but he is determined to save. So, he puts $5,000 away in his newly opened "taxes now" account. Over the course of the year, David makes a 10 percent profit, which is much higher than the average account performs. This means David's account was credited with $500, but don't forget that David has to pay taxes on this amount the same year. David feels the pinch when it is time to file his taxes; he also feels duped. His whole life he was told to save money, so he thought he was doing the right thing by placing $5,000 into a mutual fund, only to realize that so much of his profits were going to the IRS.

My clients talk to me a great deal about the feeling that they just can't get ahead: the frustration of working two jobs and doing whatever they can to scrimp and save for their futures only to realize at tax season that they will never have enough for retirement. Our whole lives we have been told to put money in the bank. That is how one saves for his or her future, but it's never that simple. The interest rate that savings accounts earn is next to nothing; as we have already discussed, they are considered "taxes now" accounts, which makes them of little use to us. If nothing else, I want readers to understand that they have to start thinking about saving differently. You have to begin questioning what you have been told your whole life.

Taxes Later

"Taxes Later" accounts are often confused with investment vehicles. While they contain investment vehicles within them, the account names distinguish their type and purpose as qualified plans from an IRS perspective. These qualified plans include:

- 401(k)s (for profit organizations);
- 403(b)s (nonprofit organizations);
- Individual Retirement Accounts (IRAs);
- Thrift Savings Plans (federal employees); and
- SEP-IRAs (self-employed business owners).

David's Story

I often say these plans are just a shell: a garage that you park investment vehicles in. If you park in the street, your vehicle will be repossessed (Taxes Now). The garage keeps your investment vehicle safe from lawsuits, liens, etc. However, this does not happen forever because, as previously mentioned, you will eventually have to pay taxes and remove your earnings from the accounts. The problem is that most people do not think far enough in advance, assuming that "Taxes Later" is better than "Taxes Now." In the end, taxes are still taxes, no matter when they hit your wallet.

These plans allow your investments to grow tax-deferred. 401(k)s are often funded with mutual funds and/or stocks. In this example, we will use a 401(k) as the "garage" holding the investment vehicle, which is a mutual fund.

Let's use our friend David as an example. David started a new job and now earns $80,000 a year. David was saving $5,000 when he was making $50,000. Now that he is earning significantly more money, he has decided to save $16,500 annually in his 401(k) garage, where he will invest it in the mutual fund account. For 2013, the IRS allows David to save up to $17,500 annually. His company will match the first 3% that he contributes which is $2,400. David is in the 25% tax bracket and will be taxed on $63,500. His taxes will be $15,875 in federal taxes. David will live off of $47,625, which is not bad for him because he was living off of $37,000 before he received his promotion and raise. The key is that the $16,500 is tax-deferred.

If David makes a 10% profit on his total contribution, including the company match of $2,400 plus his contribution of $16,500, he does not have to pay taxes on the $1,890 in interest earned because it is tax-deferred. The funds in this account are protected from creditors and liens because the IRS still has control of the account. David will not pay taxes on his withdrawals and earnings until he retires.

Essentially, the IRS will not immediately tax the money you put into these accounts. Does that sound too good to be true? It is. With these particular investment vehicles, you can't begin to utilize the money in the accounts until you are at least 59.5 years-old. If you take money out before that age, you will incur a 10 percent income tax penalty plus your tax rate at the time of withdrawal. Keep in mind that when you begin using the money from your 401(k), you will pay taxes on it. You will be in a different income bracket, but it will hurt you nonetheless.

That's not even the worst of it. Not only can you not take money out before age 59.5 without being penalized, you *have* to take money at the age of 70.5. This is what the IRS calls required minimum distribution. If you do not begin taking the money out by age 70.5, guess what happens? That's right! You'll get hit with a 50 percent tax penalty. In case it bears repeating, the IRS will *always* find a way to take what is yours.

Now, back to David:

Let's say David's job finally comes around and offers him a retirement plan. An advisor from his job-sponsored plan explains that tax-deferred plans, such as 401(k)s, are better. The advisor tells David that tax-deferred plans will accumulate more money in his retirement account; therefore, he will not have to worry about taxes until he retires and is living in a lower tax bracket.

Let's take a look at the advantages and disadvantages of tax-deferred plans:

Advantages	Disadvantages
• You are taxed later • Your taxable income is reduced • You invest before-tax dollars • You can borrow from your plan	• There is a 10 percent penalty and income tax on money taken before age 59.5 • After age 70.5, you have to start withdrawing money or suffer a 50 percent penalty • At your time of death, the money remaining in the account may be subject to estate tax • There is an age limit

Clearly, the disadvantages outweigh the advantages.

The choices that have been offered to David are tax-deferred, so he will not pay taxes on his contribution, but he will pay taxes on the profits and his contributions once he begins to use the money. The IRS allows David to take $16,500 of his yearly income and place it into one of these plans.

In my opinion, the only thing that is good about this vehicle is that David's employer matches the first three percent contribution that he makes. If your company offers this option, my advice is to only go in as much as the company will match. At the same time, consider taking advantage of the third and final concept we will discuss.

Taxes Never

"Taxes Never" means that you will never be taxed for gains when you take money out of the vehicle. Some people would argue that three vehicles are in the taxes never category: municipal bonds, Roth IRAs, and life insurance.

When my client David was faced with this real-life problem of minimizing his tax liability, he came to my office and asked what he should do. I asked him one question: do you own a Roth IRA or a life insurance policy? The answer was no.

Let's discuss the three "Taxes Never" vehicles and why the Roth IRA and life insurance policy are excellent options for David.

Municipal Bonds

Municipal bonds are used to lend money to a municipality—including states, cities and counties—and pay the investor a certain amount over a specific time period. They are not designed to create wealth but to preserve it. For example, I have a client who has amassed significant wealth and uses this vehicle as a way to preserve some of his assets and generate a certain amount of income tax-free every year.

Roth IRAs

A Roth IRA is an individual retirement account that offers tax-free income in retirement. The Roth IRA's benefit depends on your tax bracket, both now and when you retire.

David's Story

Let's take a quick look at the rules for Roth IRAs for 2013:

- They have a maximum contribution of $5,500 a year (or $6,500 a year for individuals age 50 and over), and each year the maximum is increased by the IRS;
- They cannot be used if you are single and have a modified adjusted gross income over $127,000. This amount also increases each year;
- They cannot be used if you are married, filing a joint return and the two of you have a combined modified adjusted gross income over $188,000. This increases each year; and
- Contributions must be earned income in the form of wages.

(For further qualifications, consult with your tax advisor.)

When discussing David's Roth IRA, let's use the same salary amount of $80,000. David contributes $2,400 to his 401(k) plan to take advantage of the company match. He is taxed on $77,600, leaving him with $58,200. Since David still wants to put away a total of $16,500, he will put the maximum allowed by the IRS, $5,500 in his Roth IRA after taxes. He will put the remaining $11,000 in an insurance policy for retirement purposes. I will discuss this $11,000 savings in more detail under the life insurance section.

This arrangement may not sound very different from the previous example, but because David is contributing to a Roth IRA, which is the "taxes never" concept, he gets his whole contribution and the profits, tax-free. The "taxes never" concept enables

David to grow his money tax-deferred, just like the 401(k) plan, but it also allows David to withdraw money—tax free—after he turns 59.5. If David wants to withdraw money before age 59.5, waiting five years after his initial contribution means David will suffer no penalties or taxes on the amount that he has contributed. The only downside is the IRS penalizes high-income earners. For example, if David is single in 2013 and makes more than $127,000, he cannot contribute to a Roth IRA. If David gets married in 2013 and files a joint tax return, he and his wife cannot make more than $188,000.

The Roth IRA only allows David to contribute $5,500 a year, but let's say after a few years on the job, David's new income is $127,000. This means he is now disqualified from contributing into the plan at all.

So, now let's look at the final option of the "Taxes Never" concept.

Life Insurance
David was making the same mistake that so many Americans make. David assumed that since he was not married and did not have children, he did not feel the need to put too much thought into life insurance. He had a small policy through his employer, but nothing of any consequence. The reasoning seems to be that if you do not have dependents, you do not need life insurance. That could not be further from the truth! Not only is life insurance smart to have should something happen to you and your immediate family cannot afford a funeral, but think of it this way: you are young, relatively responsibility-free, and have disposable income. Isn't this the best time to save? You can use

the money in your life insurance policy to tackle any debt you may have, or when you find that special someone, you can use the money in the policy to pay for your wedding—like I did. Again, it is time to unlearn all of the false information you have been told your whole life.

David, like many others, was also operating under the assumption that life insurance is only beneficial when you are dead. Sure, life insurance is probate-free, creditor-free, and the benefit goes to the beneficiary tax-free. But, life insurance is very much for the living.

David had a few options when it came to life insurance:

- Term Insurance—pays for a specific term and builds no cash;
- Whole Life Insurance—covers you for life, builds cash value, fixed interest rate and a fixed premium but has no premium and interest rate flexibility; and
- Universal Life Insurance—covers you for life, builds cash value, flexible premium and flexible interest rate;

David's other option was index universal life insurance. Index universal life insurance allows you to contribute as much money as you can based on your age and the size of your life insurance policy, up to the limits allowed by section 7702 of the IRS code. The most enticing aspect of this policy was the fact that David could use the money in the policy at any time without any tax penalties because he would be contributing up to his Modified Endowment Contract (MEC) limit. Essentially, this means David could take money out of his policy in the form of a loan, thus giving him the tax-free penalty option.

The maximum amount that may be put into a universal life insurance policy is based on your age, rating, and death benefit.

For details on maximum funding for life insurance, watch the following video:

http://www.webprez.com/3529/51

Let's look at how index universal life insurance applies to David. With an $80,000 annual salary, David can still save $2,400 on a pre-tax basis in his 401(k), leaving him with $77,600. He will be taxed at the 25% rate, resulting in $19,400 being paid in federal income taxes. David now has $58,200 remaining and wants to continue his additional savings of $14,100. He wants to put that $14,100 in his life insurance policy instead of his company's 401(k) plan.

Hypothetically speaking, let's assume David has built $1,000,000 cash value inside his life insurance policy. When he is ready to retire, he may begin accessing the money tax-free in the form of a loan. This is the simple explanation of the tax-free retirement benefit of index universal life insurance. It is less complicated than you thought, right?

For more insight, please view the video below:

http://www.webprez.com/3529/7

I began this chapter by telling you that it is my favorite one because I get to teach you the rules of the money game—by that, I mean learning to make tax laws work for you. The problem, of course, is that too often tax laws *do not* work for us, but knowing the specifics of how different investment vehicles work puts you at an advantage. You have to know what will work best according to your current needs, but often times, the smartest choice is opting for a life insurance policy, the only true "taxes never" option. With this option, there are no penalties for taking out money or for *not* taking out money by a certain age. Also, there are no limits on the amount you can contribute based on the face value of your policy.

In terms of finances, I like to think of life insurance the same way you would think of the foundation of a house. The base has to be solid and trustworthy because the success of the rest of the house hinges on the reliability of the foundation. The same applies to your life insurance policy. Consider it as your financial base, solid and trustworthy, the foundation your family's financial future can be built on.

Chapter 11

DAVID AND LISA'S LIFE

When holding workshops and informational sessions for American Classic Agency and my own firm, Largo Financial Services, I always make a point of discussing the financial concerns of families. In previous chapters, we have touched on the importance of teaching your children about financial responsibility as well as how you can run your family like a business. Now, I think it is important to discuss the common financial concerns families face before getting into a lesson I share with all of my clients.

Take a moment to consider these statistics:

- According to the Social Security Administration, 45 percent of 40 year-olds will experience a disability during their working years that will last 90 days or more. Before the age of 65, 80 percent of today's 20 year-olds will experience a disability that will last 90 days or more.
- According to a 2002 study from the American Savings Education Council, 46 percent of Americans have saved less

than $50,000, and 15 percent say they have saved nothing towards retirement.
- According to Life Insurance and Market Research Association (LIMRA) International, by the age of 65, the odds are nearly 1 in 2 that you will require nursing home services for at least 2.5 years.
- LIMRA International also reports that 45 percent of widows and 37 percent of widowers said their spouse had been inadequately insured.

It is important that you are aware of these facts because so many people are unprepared for the very common life events of illness, disability, nursing home services, and retirement. For many of us, these aspects of life cannot be avoided, yet we fail to plan for them. When you fail to plan, you plan to fail. Think about it: how will you make ends meet if you get injured on the job? Once you have surpassed the age where you can comfortably work, how will you live without a steady income stream? Medicare only covers a certain number of days in a nursing home or similar care facility. What happens if you need more than the days Medicare allots?

There are insurance policies that individually address all of these issues. If you purchase individual plans to meet your specific need, it can be quite expensive. For example:

- a disability policy will cost you approximately $200 a month;
- a retirement plan will be another $400;
- accelerated living benefits another $200;
- finally, life insurance another $200.

That's a whopping $1,000 a month. The average family *cannot* afford the individual policy approach, but thankfully, there is a more affordable approach, one where four unrealistic premiums become one affordable solution with living benefits.

Living benefits, also known as "accelerated benefits," are life insurance policy proceeds paid to the policyholder before they die. This benefit provides that all, or a portion of, the policy's proceeds will be paid to the policy owner when certain events occur, including:

- Terminal illness, with death expected within a specified period;
- The occurrence of a specified catastrophic illness or the need for extraordinary medical intervention, such as an organ transplant or continued life support;
- The need for long-term care due to an inability to perform a number of "activities of daily living," such as bathing, dressing, eating etc.; and
- Permanent nursing home confinement.

In these instances, the life insurance company will deduct the living benefits payment from the death benefit it ultimately pays to the beneficiary (usually at a discount).

A growing number of companies offer living benefits at no additional premium, but as the policyholder, you will be charged if and when it is used. In most cases, the company will reduce the benefits advanced to the policyholder before death to compensate for the interest it will lose on its early payout. Currently, more than 150 companies offer some type of living benefits while other companies have indicated they are developing similar plans or are considering them. It is believed that more than three million Americans are now protected by accelerated benefits.

Insurance companies usually offer anywhere between 25 to 100 percent of the death benefit as early payment, though the amount can vary among policies. Sometimes, payments are made in monthly installments; at other times, they are made in a lump sum. Some policies even allow the policyholder to choose the method of payment. You will need to consult with your insurance provider to find out the specifics of your policy.

The lesson I share with each workshop attendee is called "The Life Event Story: How Families Can Use a Living Benefits Life Insurance Policy." To illustrate the uses of a living benefits life insurance policy, I introduce a fictitious couple named David and Lisa.

Let's meet the couple:

David and Lisa are both 35 years old. They are non-smokers and have a seven-year-old son named Gerald. David and Lisa can afford to put $300 a month into a life insurance policy that has living benefits, but it has to meet their requirements. What they need is a policy that offers financial protection in the event of death, critical, chronic, or terminal illness as well as cash reserves that can be used for emergencies, college expenses, or retirement.

David and Lisa's Life

The point of this lesson is to illustrate how David and Lisa's policy works for them after a series of common life events covered by their living benefits policy.

The first life event the couple experiences occurs just one year after being issued their living benefits insurance policy: David has a heart attack. Under the critical illness rider of their policy, David has access to up to $150,000 of the critical illness benefit. He and Lisa decide to withdraw $65,000, using $15,000 for David's medical expenses and the remaining $50,000 for a down payment on a house.

Essentially, the critical illness rider provides access to the money in your policy should a serious, life-threatening event occur, such as a stroke, a heart attack, or kidney disease. In these situations, like David and Lisa, the family can choose how much money (up to the limit) they would like to take out of their policy to address the issue. Some of you may be wondering, "What does putting a down payment on a house have to do with a critical illness?" Let's say David and Lisa were looking to purchase a home around the time David had a heart attack. Having a living benefits policy means you do not have to put your life on hold when sickness strikes. Life happens, and this policy provides access to funds to pay medical expenses and continue with any plans you had prior to the illness.

I cannot convey to you how life saving these benefits are. I have seen with my own eyes how they have helped people keep a roof over their heads and food on their table when unexpected illness strikes. For example, a client of mine was diagnosed with cancer. She was a humble school bus driver who lost her job while she was undergoing treatment for her cancer. Because of her living benefits policy, she was able to withdraw $70,000 from her policy, which she used to pay her bills, her mortgage, and keep herself clothed and fed until she was well enough to seek employment once again. Without this policy, she would have surely lost her house.

Let's get back to our story:

Fifteen years into the policy, David and Lisa experience their second major life event: their son Gerald goes to college. The couple uses the cash value in their policy to help pay for college expenses, providing their son with $5,000 a year for four years.

When David and Lisa turn 65, they experience their next major life event—one too few Americans are prepared for: retirement. When David and Lisa retire, their policy has a combined cash value of $225,000. They are able to stop paying premiums and take $50,000 in cash from David's policy for a down payment on a vacation condo.

At age 79, Lisa becomes chronically ill and enters a nursing home. Because of this latest life event, the insurance company accelerates one percent of her Death Benefit each month. The monthly benefit is $2,200 per month, and over the course of 60 months, this adds up to $132,000.

Four years later when David is 83, he is diagnosed with congestive heart failure and is not expected to live longer than two

David and Lisa's Life

years. By this time, the Death Benefit in his policy has grown to $650,000. David and Lisa decide to accelerate $250,000 of the Death Benefit, receiving $235,000. After medical expenses ($85,000), they give $150,000 to their son, Gerald, who will use the money to purchase a home for his family.

A year later, David and Lisa both pass away at age 86. The remaining death benefit of $630,000 is reserved for their grandchildren's college fund. Let's break the story of David and Lisa down into numbers to give you a better understanding of what transpired in this lesson: David and Lisa each contributed a monthly amount of $150 to their policy (for a total of $300 a month).

When David had his heart attack (a critical illness), the couple withdrew $65,000.

- Medical expenses: $15,000
- Down payment on home: $50,000

Gerald's college fund (policy cash): $20,000

David and Lisa retire (policy cash):

Condo down payment: $50,000

Lisa enters a nursing home (chronic illness): $132,000

David's heart failure (terminal illness):

- Medical expenses: $85,000
- Gerald's homes $150,000

Lisa's death (remaining life insurance):

- Grandchildren's college: $630,000

When adding up the numbers, this means the total benefits paid to David and Lisa were $1,132,000: $502,000 in living benefits and $630,000 in death benefits. Over the course of 51 years, the couple only paid $108,000 in premiums, which means their return was more than 10 times what they put into the policy.

Clearly, this is life changing money, and it is money that the average family could have access to if they planned properly. Again, once you know better, you do better and now that you are aware of how these policies work, there is no excuse not to begin setting the wheels in motion for generational wealth.

It is not just about creating wealth, however. What happens if you become ill? What would your family do without the benefit of a living benefits policy? If you do not think your family could lose everything, think again.

According to a 2009 Harvard Medical School study, 60 percent of 1.5 million Americans who go bankrupt are actually capsized by medical bills. The study found that bankruptcies due to medical bills increased by nearly 50 percent in a six-year period, from 46 percent in 2001 to 62 percent in 2007; most of those who filed for bankruptcy were middle-class, well-educated homeowners.

We have already learned of the disappearing middle class and the racial wealth gap, so needless to say, these numbers are even direr for communities of color, low-income communities, or those who did not graduate from college. Steffie Woolhandler, one of the authors of the study, says the average American is "one illness away from financial ruin in this country."

I do not share this to scare you but to illustrate the very real danger that you and your family are up against. If you have no money saved in case of an emergency, a life insurance policy with living benefits becomes so much more important than creating generational wealth: it is the difference between your family surviving through your illness and your family facing financial ruin. I cannot reiterate this enough: when you approach an agent about obtaining a life insurance policy, make sure you discuss living benefits. It can make all the difference in the world for your family.

Chapter 12

A CONVERSATION WITH THE AUTHOR

What is most gratifying about the work you do?
My mission is to help clients discover their path toward wealth and financial independence by improving their financial intelligence. The most gratifying part of what I do is helping people change their lives when it comes to their finances. Everyone works, for one reason or another, to make a living and take care of his or her family. The good thing is they are making money, but the bad thing is they don't understand the rules to the money game. I enjoy helping folks and showing them how to accomplish that goal, which is to make sure their family gets what they want them to have in the end. When it comes to the advisors I recruit or train, I help them earn the income they desire and educate them on how money works. Helping folks secure their financial futures by using a pragmatic, common sense approach is what truly drives me.

What would you say is the biggest challenge when it comes to getting individuals and families to invest in creating generational wealth?
I think part of the challenge is trying to break the myth of not being able to attain wealth. Most people don't see themselves positioned for wealth or have already lost hope. The people they see around them are not speaking their language. A lot of times the challenge is trying to teach them a different way of thinking. Most people are accustomed to doing the same thing over and over again, so they feel it is the right way. In some cases, people simply do what everyone else is doing and assume it is okay. But the way they have been taught is not necessarily the right way. The challenging part is trying to show them a different way to look at things, especially when it comes to insurance. Most people do not see insurance as a tool that can create generational wealth because they have been told that it's just for death, so they do not understand the power of it. It is a matter of breaking that myth and concept people have.

We are uncomfortable talking with our children about wealth. Why don't we talk with our children about wealth? Because no one talks to the parents. Financial experts only talk about stocks and real estate. That's fine but not everyone can invest in them. The wealthy do not buy stocks to retire off of. They buy stocks and real estate to hold and transfer to their children from one generation to the next.

What would you say is the greatest lesson you have learned in this business?
The greatest lesson I have learned is knowing there is so much out there to learn. You cannot stay in the same lane all of your

life. You have to continually study, understand, and want to grow. Also, surround yourself with people who are a whole lot better than you in terms of knowledge, especially financial knowledge. You can never stop learning. If you want to achieve something when it comes to financial wealth, all of the information you need is publicly available, but you have to seek and find the right people who are willing to help guide you.

What are some of the ways you continue developing and learning more about your business and industry?
The industry provides continuing education. Other than that, I continually research and learn about people who have already proven that they have done well financially. I study and learn what they have done and how they have done it. I continually learn about the industry and make sure I know about new ideas, tax laws, or anything that impacts wealth growth. I try to stay ahead of the curve. I network with very successful financial advisors who are doing the things I want to do and learn from them.

Who is your role model?
Jerry Policastro, Founder and CEO of American Classic Agency (parent company of Largo Financial Services), is a man I have admired for many years. That is the reason I requested that he write the foreword to this book. He is a man of integrity and is committed to excellence. Jerry cares a lot about people and will do anything to make sure his agents are successful. In the financial services industry, many leaders view their financial advisors as just a number and are only concerned with how much money they can make for them. Jerry genuinely cares. I am only

one of thousands of agents who feel that way. A lot of us have been with him for more than 14 years. That says a lot about the kind of person he is, especially in an industry where many advisors move on after five years or less. Thus, he has been very successful in establishing American Classic Agency.

What motivated you to write this book?
The first reason is that, when leading seminars, attendees always asked me if I had a book containing the information that I shared. They would often say, "You should write a book about that." I did not want to write just any kind of book. I wanted to provide a resource that would impact people, particularly when I noticed there is so much information out there, especially the basic information that people do not know. I do not think my book is the one and only resource, but it will give readers a start and get them thinking. I cannot reach the masses through seminars; however, if I write and publish, I can reach the masses much easier, at least those who want the information, and they may pass it on to others.

The second reason is I want my children, grandchildren, and generations that follow them to understand that their inherited wealth did not come easily. We sometimes hear stories of that one child in a wealthy family who questions why they have wealth and others who do not, without considering how that wealth was established. I do not want that one child in my family to take his wealth for granted, rebel against the family, and forget that the person who made it happen worked hard and sacrificed a lot. I want those children to have a historical perspective. They must understand that their great-great-great grandfather was an immigrant from Africa who came into a country, worked hard, earned everything he had—he was not given anything—and understand why he did what he did.

What is the biggest compliment you have received from a client?
I never really look for compliments, but I enjoy seeing a client get it. I love explaining something to them and seeing that it just makes sense. I remember a gentleman once saying that he knew there was something else that he could do, but he just did not know what it was. He said I completed the puzzle for him and helped him tremendously. He had always asked other people, but they could not answer his questions. He was so grateful.

What is the biggest compliment you have received from an advisor?
They tell me they appreciate the fact I am very helpful and I inspire them with my work ethic. I am willing to help them and give 100% to those who are willing to learn and work hard to make sure they achieve their goals. I am a believer that whatever I do, God will reward me. I do not depend so much on what others tell me.

What do you think your readers would be most surprised to know about you?
I am just a regular guy from West Africa with a high school diploma who had the will to be successful. I did not come from a family where my dad had the money to send me abroad to school. Early in my financial career, I decided to start understanding the business beyond simply making money. I needed to understand what wealthy people do. In Nigeria, a lot of people's wealth dies with them. In the United States, you see

the same trend, but there are wealthy people who transfer their wealth, like the Kennedys and Rockefellers.

I pray for God's guidance. I remember when I was 18, I said that I wanted to be a millionaire at 25. I know God smiled and said, "Yeah right! If I give you $50,000, what are you going to do with it? You'd probably blow through it." What He *did* was set the path, and at age 24, I began following that path. It was not easy, but I stayed the course and continued even when it was tough. I kept going and going. Today, as God would have it because it is all God's plan, this is what I do—this is *all* I do. Most people want to focus on multiple streams of income without building a solid foundation first. Donald Trump uses his real estate foundation to help him do other things. The real estate foundation is first.

What brings you fulfillment outside of work?
I am fulfilled by spending time with family, enjoying them, and seeing the reason why I do what I do every day.

What else would you like to share with your readers about who you are?
When they read this book, I want people to know that even though I know that I do not know all of the answers when it comes to creating generational wealth, I DO know that it is working for me, and you will see the results. I am just a guy who came into an opportunity that was given to me. I was waiting tables at IHOP at age 24. I came into the country without knowing anything about it. I left Africa at 18 and went to a foreign land. I went to Canada and then came to the U.S. I got into the

financial services industry without even knowing a whole lot about what I was getting into, but I stayed focused because I saw the possibilities and knew a lot of people needed financial education.

The information I was learning was not being taught in schools and universities. They teach everything else but not how to properly plan for long-term wealth. We focus on accumulating money, but no one is telling us how to keep the money. This same was true for me as a young man with no financial knowledge who was a consumer like everyone else. I decided to step outside the box and saw the opportunity in this financial services business. I was able to do things for my parents and take care of them financially. That drives me. I continued learning the industry and finding out there was a whole lot of information out there that no one is actually taking the time to share with everyday people on a personal level. I have always loved helping people, working with them, and seeing them do better.

I just want people to understand that, after reading this book, you might say to yourself, "I don't know if it's too late." The key is I want you to sit down with your family and have that money conversation, which is something we do not do often. The wealthy do it. They have those conversations and talk about how to continue growing the family wealth; then they seek ways to do it. They bring in trusted advisors to continually teach them how to grow the wealth. I believe a family is a business. The husband is the president, the wife is the vice president, and the children are the workers. Just like a business has bills, a family has bills. Just as businesses have income, families have income. As a business looks at how to increase profit every year, families need to think about how to increase family profits every year. Just like businesses think about how we want our business to grow from one year to another and stay in business for years and years, that's the same way families need to look at the family wealth. You want it to grow from one generation to the next generation.

What I want you to take away is that this is a book to get you to start thinking differently from the way you were thinking before you picked up my book. I hope the book gives you that "aha" moment. I don't expect you to agree with everything in the book, and I am sure some people will advise you otherwise, yet I am hoping the simplicity with which I share the information will help you. You have nothing to lose…just try it. You don't have to put 100% of your money in it, but put at least 10% in and try the ideas I have given. The worst case scenario is you die and leave your family with some money. If you do not die in the near term, at least you are walking away with tax-free cash for your retirement. Either way, you will benefit now and for generations to come.

Appendix
KEY TERMS & DEFINITIONS

401(k): A 401(k) plan is the common name in the U.S. for a tax-qualified, defined-contribution account. Under the plan, retirement savings contributions are provided (and sometimes proportionately matched) by an employer, deducted from the employee's paycheck before taxation (therefore tax-deferred until withdrawn during retirement), and limited to a maximum annual contribution of $17,500 as of 2013. There are catch-up provisions available.

403(b): A 403(b) plan is a U.S. tax-advantaged retirement savings plan available for public education organizations, some non-profit employers, cooperative hospital service organizations, and self-employed ministers. It has tax treatment similar to a 401(k) plan, especially after the Economic Growth and Tax Relief Reconciliation Act of 2001. Employee salary deferrals into a 403(b) plan are made before income tax is paid and allowed to grow tax-deferred until the money is taxed as income when withdrawn from the plan.

Annuity: An annuity contract is created when an insured party, usually an individual, pays a life insurance company a single premium that will later be distributed back to the insured party over time.

Articles of incorporation: The "Articles of Incorporation" (sometimes also referred to as the Certificate of Incorporation or the Corporate Charter) are the primary rules governing the management of a corporation in the United States and Canada and are filed with a state or other regulatory agency.

Assets: In financial accounting, an asset is an economic resource. Anything tangible or intangible that is capable of being owned or controlled to produce value and that is held to have positive economic value is considered an asset. Simply stated, assets represent value of ownership that can be converted into cash (although cash itself is also considered an asset).

Bank-Owned Life Insurance: A form of life insurance purchased by banks where the bank is the beneficiary and/or owner.

Bankruptcy: Bankruptcy is a legal status of a person or other entity that cannot repay the debts it owes to creditors.

Bond: A bond is an instrument of indebtedness of the bond issuer to the holders. It is a debt security, under which the issuer owes the holders a debt and, depending on the terms of the bond, is obliged to pay them interest and/or to repay the principal at a later date.

Business loan: A bank loan granted for the use of a business.

Buy sell agreement: A buy–sell agreement, also known as a buyout agreement, is a legally binding agreement between co-owners of a business that governs the situation if a co-owner dies or is otherwise forced to leave the business or chooses to leave the business.

Capital: Capital goods, real capital, or capital assets are already-produced durable goods or any non-financial asset that is used in production of goods or services.

Capital gains: A profit from the sale of property or of an investment.

Capital stock: The common and preferred stock a company is authorized to issue, according to their corporate charter.

Captive organizations: Captive organizations primarily provide insurance to the parent organization that created them. These organizations act as a legal veil that protects their parent in the event of a large insurance payout while other businesses simply want to use captives to keep insurance segregated from their main business for liability purposes.

C corporation: C corporation refers to any corporation that, under United States federal income tax law, is taxed separately from its owners.

Certificate of Deposit (CD) account: A certificate of deposit (CD) is a time deposit, a financial product commonly sold in the United States by banks, thrift institutions, and credit unions.

Checking account: A transactional deposit account held at a financial institution that allows for withdrawals and deposits. Money held in a checking account is very liquid and can be withdrawn using checks, automated cash machines and electronic debits, among other methods.

Corporation-Owned Life Insurance: Corporate-owned life insurance (COLI) is life insurance on employees' lives that is owned by the employer, with benefits payable to the employer.

Certificate of incorporation: A certificate of incorporation is a legal document relating to the formation of a company or corporation. It is a license to form a corporation issued by state government.

Charitable trust: A charitable trust is an irrevocable trust established for charitable purposes.

Corporation: A corporation is a separate legal entity that has been incorporated under state law.

CPA: Certified Public Accountant (CPA) is the statutory title of qualified accountants in the United States who have passed the Uniform Certified Public Accountant Examination and have met additional state education and experience requirements for certification as a CPA.

Creditors: A creditor is a party (e.g. person, organization, company, or government) that has a claim on the services of a second party.

Death benefits: The amount on a life insurance policy that is payable to the beneficiary when the insured passes away.

Debt: A debt is an obligation owed by one party (the debtor) to a second party, (the creditor), usually this refers to assets granted by the creditor to the debtor, but the term can also be used metaphorically to cover moral obligations and other interactions not based on economic value.

Dividend: A dividend is a payment made by a corporation to its shareholders, usually as a distribution of profits.

Entrepreneur: An entrepreneur is an individual who organizes and operates a business or businesses, taking on financial risk to do so.

Equal Pay Act: The Equal Pay Act of 1963 is a United States federal law amending the Fair Labor Standards Act, aimed at abolishing wage disparity based on sex. It was signed into law on June 10, 1963, by John F. Kennedy as part of his New Frontier Program.

Estate: An estate is the net worth of a person at any point in time.

Estate tax: The Estate Tax is a tax on the transfer of property at your death. It consists of an accounting of everything you own or have certain interests in at the date of death.

Family limited partnership: Family Limited Partnerships (commonly called FLPs) are frequently used to move wealth from one generation to another. Partners are either General Partners (GP) or Limited Partners (LP). One or more General Partners are responsible for managing the FLP and its assets.

Family trust: A trust where the beneficiaries and/or their entitlements to the trust fund are not fixed but are determined by the criteria set out in the trust instrument by the settlor.

Federal Perkins Loan: The Federal Perkins Loan Program provides low interest loans to help needy students finance the costs of postsecondary education. Students attending any one of approximately 1,700 participating postsecondary institutions can obtain Perkins loans from the school.

Federal income taxes: A tax levied by the United States Internal Revenue Service (IRS) on the annual earnings of individuals, corporations, trusts, and other legal entities.

Financial advisor: A financial adviser is a professional who renders financial services to clients.

Gender wage gap: The difference between male and female earnings expressed as a percentage of male earnings.

Key Terms & Definitions

Gift tax: The gift tax is a tax on the transfer of property by one individual to another while receiving nothing, or less than full value, in return. The tax applies whether the donor intends the transfer to be a gift or not.

Heir: A person legally entitled to the property or rank of another on that person's death.

Income tax: An income tax is a tax on individual earnings (income) that is paid to the government.

Incorporation: The forming of a new corporation (a corporation being a legal entity that is effectively recognized as a person under the law). The corporation may be a business, a nonprofit organization, sports club, or a government of a new city or town.

Inheritance: Inheritance is the practice of passing on property, titles, debts, rights, and obligations upon the death of an individual.

Interest: Interest is a fee paid by a borrower of assets to the owner as a form of compensation for the use of the assets.

Internal Revenue Service: The IRS is the U.S. government agency responsible for tax collection and tax law enforcement.

Investment vehicle: A product used by investors with the intention of having positive returns. Investment vehicles can be low-risk, such as certificates of deposit (CDs) or bonds, or can carry a greater degree of risk such as with stocks, options, and futures. Other types of investment vehicles include annuities, collectibles (art or coins, for example), mutual funds, and exchange-traded funds (ETFs).

IRA: An Individual Retirement Account is a form of "individual retirement plan," [2] provided by many financial institutions, that provides tax advantages for retirement savings in the United States.

Liability: In financial accounting, a liability is defined as an obligation of an entity arising from past transactions or events, the settlement of which may result in the transfer or use of assets, provision of services or other yielding of economic benefits in the future.

Lien: In law, a lien is a form of security interest granted over an item of property to secure the payment of a debt or performance of some other obligation.

Lilly Ledbetter Fair Pay Act: The Act amends the Civil Rights Act of 1964. The new act states that the 180-day statute of limitations for filing an equal-pay lawsuit regarding pay discrimination resets with each new paycheck affected by that discriminatory action.

Liquidity: The degree to which an asset or security can be bought or sold in the market without affecting the asset's price.

Living benefits: An advance cash payment of part of the amount of insurance prior to the death of the insured person for certain conditions as defined in the policy. It provides financial assistance to the insured person while still living.

LLC: A limited liability company (LLC) is a flexible form of enterprise that blends elements of partnership and corporate structures. An LLC is not a corporation; it is a legal form of company that provides limited liability to its owners in the vast majority of United States jurisdictions.

LLP: A limited liability partnership (LLP) is a partnership in which some or all partners (depending on the jurisdiction) have limited liabilities. It therefore exhibits elements of partnerships and corporations.

Mutual fund: A mutual fund is a type of professionally managed collective investment vehicle that pools money from many investors to purchase securities.

Partnership: A partnership is the relationship existing between two or more persons who join to carry on a trade or business.

Paycheck Fairness Act: The Paycheck Fairness Act is legislation twice introduced and twice rejected by the United States Congress to expand the scope of the Equal Pay Act of 1963 and the Fair Labor Standards Act as part of an effort to address male–female income disparity in the United States. A Census Bureau report published in 2008 indicated that women's median annual earnings were 77.5 percent of men's earnings, a disparity attributed to systematic discrimination against women and women's lifestyle choices.

Permanent life insurance: Permanent life insurance is a term sometimes used for life insurance, such as whole life or endowment, where the sum assured is due to be paid out at the end of the policy (assuming the policy is kept current) and the policy accrues a cash value.

Personal loan: A personal loan is borrowing a sum of money from a financial institution for personal use. Individuals may use the money for almost anything; some examples are a vacation, a car, home improvements or bill consolidation.

Probate court: A probate court (also called a surrogate court) is a specialized court that deals with matters of probate and the administration of estates. Probate courts administer proper distribution of the assets of a decedent (one who has died), adjudicates the validity of wills, enforces the provisions of a valid will (by issuing the grant of probate), prevents malfeasance by executors and administrators of estates, and provides for the equitable distribution of the assets of persons who die intestate (without a valid will), such as by granting a grant of administration giving judicial approval to the personal representative to administer matters of the estate.

Proprietorship: A business structure in which an individual and his/her company are considered a single entity for tax and liability purposes.

Qualified plans: A plan that meets requirements of the Internal Revenue Code and, as a result, is eligible to receive certain tax benefits.

Racial wealth gap: Vast differences in wealth across racial groups in the United States. The wealth gap between white and African-American families nearly tripled from $85,000 in 1984 to $236,500 in 2009.

Savings account: Saving accounts are accounts maintained by retail financial institutions that pay interest but cannot be used directly as money in the narrow sense of a medium of exchange.

Savings bond: A bond issued by the government and sold to the general public.

S corporation: S corporations are corporations that elect to pass corporate income, losses, deductions, and credit through to their shareholders for federal tax purposes.

SEP-IRAs: A Simplified Employee Pension Individual Retirement Arrangement (SEP IRA) is a variation of the Individual Retirement Account used in the United States. SEP IRAs are adopted by business owners to provide retirement benefits for the business owners and their employees. There are no significant administration costs for a self-employed person with no employees. If the self-employed person does have employees, all employees must receive the same benefits under a SEP plan. Since SEP accounts are treated as IRAs, funds can be invested the same way as any other IRA.

Shareholders: A shareholder or stockholder is an individual or institution (including a corporation) that legally owns a share of stock in a public or private corporation.

State taxes: State Income taxes, which vary by state, are a percentage of money that you pay to the state government based on the income you make at your job.

Stocks: A type of security that signifies ownership in a corporation and represents a claim on part of the corporation's assets and earnings.

Supplemental Executive Retirement Plan: A non-qualified retirement plan for key company employees, such as executives, that provides benefits above and beyond those covered in other retirement plans such as IRA, 401(k) or NQDC plans. There are many different kinds of SERPs available to companies wishing to ensure that their key employees are able to maintain their current standards of living in retirement.

Tax advisor: A tax advisor is a financial expert especially trained in tax law.

Tax bracket: Tax brackets are the divisions at which tax rates change in a progressive tax system.

Tax-deferred: Tax deferred refers to instances where a taxpayer can delay paying taxes to some future period.

Treasuries: Negotiable U.S. Government debt obligations, backed by its full faith and credit. The U.S. government issues treasuries in order to pay for government projects. The money paid out for a Treasury bond is essentially a loan to the government.

Trust: A trust is a relationship whereby property is held by one party for the benefit of another. A trust is created by a settlor, who transfers some or all of his or her property to a trustee. The trustee holds that property for the trust's beneficiaries.

Universal life insurance: Universal life insurance is a type of permanent life insurance, primarily in the United States of America. Under the terms of the policy, the excess of premium payments above the current cost of insurance is credited to the cash value of the policy. The cash value is credited each month with interest, and the policy is debited each month by a cost of insurance charge.

Will: A will or testament is a legal declaration by which a person, the testator, names one or more persons to manage his or her estate and provides for the distribution of his property at death.

ADDITIONAL RESOURCES

Pension Plan—412(e)(3)
http://www.webprez.com/3529/45

Executive Bonus Plan
http://www.webprez.com/3529/41

Home Equity Transfer
http://www.webprez.com/3529/1

Long-term Care
http://www.webprez.com/3529/8

Section 79 Plan
http://www.webprez.com/3529/13

SPECIAL RECOGNITION

Key contributors to my book project

LaFern K. Batie, MBA—Project Consultant
The Batie Group, LLC

Vernetta Williams, Ph.D., Editor
Chrysalis Consulting, LLC

Shyamie Dixit, Attorney, Reviewer
Dixit Law Firm

Susan Hightower, CPA, Reviewer
Jireh Tax and Accounting Services

Tina Vasquez, Contributor

Kevette Kane, Contributor

Daria Awusah, Contributor

Creating Generational Wealth®

Professionals with whom I have worked and crossed paths throughout my financial services career

Vera Abanda	Yolanda Anglin
Abraham Abich	Akeem Applewhite
Anthony Abrams	Jermaine Armstrong
Reginald Abrams	Justin Arnold
Gorden Achu	Gary Artis
Constance Achu Mokom	Loretta Asata McLean
Clarence Adams	Cathy Atkins
Adedayo Adeneye	Kwami Attipoe
Christopher Adeniyi	Athanasius Awasom
Abidemi Adetutu	Gabriela Ayala
James Afueh	Frances Ayeh-Kumi
Michael Agetstein	Babatunde Ayokunle
Alexander Agiliga	Patricia Ayuk
Frank Aikens	Mohamed Bah
Alex Akporji	Donald Bailey
MD Alam	Julius Baker
Clifford Alexander	Nathaniel Banks
Gage Alexander	Shanice Barker
Delby Allen	Dana Barnes
Douglas Allen	Eidu Barnes
Kimberly Allen	DanYelle Batts
Alwyn Alli	Garry Batts
Ivan Alvarenga	Reynold Beache
Jean-Robert Anantua	Damien Beal
Brandon Anderson	Meloneese Beal
Gregory Anderson	Lynn Beamon
Victoria Anderson	Dennis Becton

Special Recognition

Arthur Bellows
David Belton
Sharon Ben-David
Phillip Bernhardt
Muhammad Bin-Ansari
Patrice Blackman
Hugh Blackwell
Sharanda Blakey
Sona Bokassah
Sandra Bonaparte
Cynthia Bond
Demia Bond
Darryl Bonner
Sharon Borders-Chittams
Felecia Bowles
Evelyn Bowser
James Boyd
Bayo Braimoh
Brian Braxton
Roseann Bricker
Nathan Bright
Dominique Broadway
Gloria Brown
Rico Brown
Rochelle Brown
Charles Brown, Jr.
Adrienne Bryant
Canisha Bryant
T Bryant
Connie Buckley

Darian Buggs
Bessie Burley
James Burrell
Clinton Burton
John Bush
Jessica Bustinza
Joanne Butler
Lois Butler
Daisy Calderon
Chasity Caldwell
Kevin Callahan
Alexander Canseco
Brene Carrington
Harvey Carroll
Kevin Carter
Marques Carter
Zina Carter
Michael Cartwright
Geoffrey Cash
Raisa Castillo
Rhonda Cauthen
Linda Chalk-Watts
Robert Champion
Miyesha Chappell
Antonio Cheeks
David Chesley
Michael Cipriani
Tanya Claggett
Darius Clair
Edwina Clark

Dana Cleaborn
Oluwaseun Cole
Darrell Coleman
Jerrell Coleman
Natasha Coleman
Breanna Colon
Gregory Cooper
Benjamin Copeland
Sheila Copeland
Eric Cornnor
Angela Corprew
Lamont Corprew
Eva Corpus
Roland Coston
Braulio Cotera
Sherita Cotten
Angelique Cox
Xiomara Crespo
Rebecca Cross
Cawarnest Cruse
Merlin Cruz
Ashley Culpeper
Kay Culpeper
Kierra Culpeper
Tony Cummings
John Cunningham
Ernest Cunningham, Jr.
Joseph Curtis
Carmen Cutrone
Camisha Dabney

Maxine Daniely
Chad Darden
Jacqueline Davenport
Yvonne Davis
Shewatsehai Debebe
Deborah DeFlorimonte
Evelyn Deflorimonte
Tavon Dempsey
Ozgun Deniz
Lesly Derenoncourt
Iby Diaz
Aaron Dixon
Shelley Dodson
Koffi Dossou
Linnell Dowling
Marc Dozier
Marlon Dubon
Rosa Dubon
Larae Dudley
Karen Dulysse
Shelly Dunaway
James Duncan
Richard Dunn
Yvonne Dunwell
Houng Duong
Douglas Eason
Brian Easter
Kevin Edmondson
Donald Edwards
Jeanine Edwards

Special Recognition

Joseph Edwards
Prosper Ehunyi
Caleb Ekane
Andrew Ekunseitan
Georgiaett Ellington
Deborah Emerson
Etheldreda Enongene
Evaristus Enongene
Miguel Enongene
Manuel Enriquez
Joseph Espaillat
Caroline Estime
Cand Evans
Terri Evans
James Evering
Daniel Evertsz
Daniel Ewuoso
Alice Eyong
Douglas Eze
Fisayo Fakunle
Sunday Faleye
Jamie Farmer
Habeeb Fasuyi
Helen Ferguson
Raisa Fernandez
Jeanne Fields
Maria Figueroa
O'Dowd Fleming
Emmanuel Fomukong
George Fon

Celestine Fondungallah
James Fonge
Marshall Forrester
Betrand Fote
David Fowler
Rony Francois
George Fraser
Heather Fraser
Daniel Freshley
Ken Friend
Clinton Frye
Joe Garbaravage
Natalie Garcia
Phillip Garris
Tanya Gibson
Charles Gilbert
Rolanda Gilkie-Carrethers
Sheilah Gill
Lara Gillette
Keith Gilliard
Anna Godfrey
Erik Goerman
Leonore Goerman
Scot Goldstein
Rita Gomez
Blanca Gonzales
Kimberly Graham
Michelle Grant
Telaya Grant
Dwight Graves

Julette Gray
Charles Green
Melvin Green
Sabrina Green
Cynthia Greene
Ronisha Greenfield
Jonathan Gregory
Kevin Griffith
Betty Gross
Renee Guelce
Dexter Gumbs
Virginia Gunthrop
Chantal Gwannulla
Mbongeh Gwanvala
Casey Hall
Dorothy Hall
Patrick Halton
Hazel Hamilton
Bradley Hanke
Corey Hankerson
Hosea Hardin
William Harper
Andre Harris
Angela Harris
Moise Harris
Percy Harris
LaTraviete Hawley
Michael Hayes
Timothy Helbling
Donna Heslop Adams

Brittany Hicks
Katherine Higginbotham
Susan Hightower
Elaine Hill
Sylvia Hill
Sonya Hinds
Linda Hinton
Turiya Hodge
Thea Holeyfield Lewis
Aravia Holloman
Barbara Holmes
Marcia Holmes-Maye
Charles Holson
Denise Hopkins
Audrey Hosley
Shajuania Howard
Timothy Howard
Fan-Jye Hsu
Kelli Hubbard
Nila Hughes
Pamela Humphrey
Peter Hundley
Omar Ibrahim
Obidimpka Ikezuagu
Emma Ikokwu
Dennis Ishicheli
Joseph Itoe
Isofi Itomi
Nicole Jabo
Andrew Jackson

Special Recognition

Cheryl Jackson
Janet Jackson
Michella Jackson
Tyrone Jackson
Monique Jacobs
Brenda Jamison
David Janiczek
Sheila Jardine
Emmanuel Jean Pierre
Claudia Jeffers
Starr Jefferson
Christopher Jenkins
Holly Jenkins
Ronald Jennings
James Jernigan
David Johnson
Derrick Johnson
Eric Johnson
Gregory Johnson
James Johnson
Michael Johnson
Pervis Johnson
Rodolfo Johnson
Shandel Johnson
Angela Jones
Brannon Jones
Brenda Jones
Kevin Jones
Michael B. Jones
Reginald Jones

Wayne Jones
Angela Julian
John Kaendera
Bernadette Kamara
James Katzaman
Shawnice Kearney
Bettie Kelley
Jeremy Kelly
Christopher Kemper
Renard Kerr
Linus Ketcha
Bonnie Kidd
Archie King
Ronald King
Richard Klesyk
Todd Knickel
Stephon Knox
Jean Ko Ko Gyi
Akossiwa Kolani El
Hadiatu Koroma
Lisa Kosh
Alease Kouadio
Louis Kressaty
John Krueger
Libe Kunz
Milvia Lagarda
Thomas Lakin
Kimberly Lambert
Samuel Laneave
Pepa Lanham

Troy LaPrade
Ashorobi Lateef
Patricia Latimore
Patrice Lea-Njike
Yvonne Lee
Maria Legrande
Adona Leonard
Gerald Leonard
Katrina Leonard
Betty Lewis
Chicquita Lewis
David Lewis
Edith Lewis
Keith Lewis
Linda Lewis
Lucy Lewis
Michael Ligons
Lee Linder
Glenda Lloyd Rogers
Cindy Lockard
Catherine Longonje
Gary Lord
Durshon Louallen
Candyce Love
Jetaun Lowery
Tonya Lowery
Ellen Lux
Calvin Mack
Kevin Mack
Tessa Magyar

Frederick Makinde
Eleonore Mandengue
Margaret Mann
Alusine Mansaray
Brad Martin
Louis Martin
William Massenburg
Curtis May
Angela Mayo
Deborah Mayo
Karyn McAdory
Monta McAdory
Monica McCants
James McCartney
Derrick McClellan
Parker McDaniel
Shawn McDonald
Lakecia McFadden
Vernee McFarlin
Michael McGuire
Kianna McMillan
Gerald McNair
Erika McNeal
Kezon McNeill
James Mead
Alfredo Melendez
Kasimma Melendez
William Mellon
Sherry Melton
Renato Mendez

Special Recognition

Elmer Merino
D Michael
Larrne Midgett Lancaster
Pamela Miles
Mary Miller
Marlon Milton
Ashli Mitchell
Ellen Mitchell
Janice Mitchell
Michael Mitchell, Sr.
Edward Mokam
Beverly Moore
Kevin Moore
Monica Moore
Suezanne Moore
Tiffany Moore
Terry Moore, Jr.
Terry Moore, Sr.
Kevin Moravek
Charville Morgan
Vinara Mosby
John Mshimba
Lonnie Myers
Edward Najjar
Aaron Nash
Aleazor Nash
Scarlene Ndandjeu Mbanga
Demba Ndiaye
Gilbert Ndip
Bertha Ndoh

Robert Nero
Timothy Nero
Paul Newman
Marcel Ngue
Duy Nguyen
Peter Nguyen
Gabriel Nyobe
Julius Oben
Emmanuel Obi
Alexander Obodo
Joan Oboite
Charles O'Connor
Hans Ofulue
Lincoln O'Gilvie
Ayuk Ojong
Michael Okolo
Grace Olabosipo
Theophilus Oladipo
Patricia Olaleye
Akinnuga Olusanya
Lawrence Omerennah
Cyril-Westcot Omwirhiren
Ihuoma Onyeso-Nwachukwu
Kenneth Opara
Beverly Owens
Bob Owens
Derek Owens
Jason Owens
Rowen Owens
Hansen Padmore

Creating Generational Wealth®

Robert Paige
Anthony Parham
Sheridan Parker
Vaught Parker
Corey Parrish
Jacqueline Patrick
Betty Pearson
Cherie Pellum
Jorge Pena
Joyce Pendleton
Jeffrey Pennington
Juan Perez
Kairene Perry
Pamela Person
Venus Peterson
Constantine Petropoulos
Mary Phelps
Pamela Piper
Daughan Pitts
Monica Poe
Damon Pollard
Adekunle Popoola
Kevin Posey
Jarrard Powell
Emmanuel Pressley
Kenneth Preston
Craig Price
Mushiya Pulanco
Walter Raines
Rashish Ramcharan

Lauren Randall
Jernaria Reynolds
Carolyn Rice
George Rice
Jonathan Rice
Catherine Richardson
Kwame Richardson
Philip Richardson
Anthony Ricks
Michael Riconscente
Damon Ridley
Brian Riley
Edward Riley
Reginald Riley, Jr.
Theodore Robinson
Darren Rochester
Bennie Rogers
Jeffrey Rogers
Monique Rogers
Howard Rose
Armeta Ross
Mark Ross
Harold Rowson
Emily Rucker
Rosalyn Russell
Valney Russell
Vincent Ryu
Kay Salau
Ericka Sallee
Ernest Sallee

Special Recognition

Tammy Sallee
Lavon Sampson
Pablo Sanchez
Theresa Sanders
Tiffany Sanders
Adeline Sandy
Scout Saylors
Mary Scopin
Susan Scott
Tyreece Scott
Ted Scotton
Stacey Seim
Bobby Semple
Valarie Senatus
Marques Sewell
Syed Shah
Michael Shannon
Jason Sharpe
Dianah Shaw
Fannie Sheahin
William Sheldon
Jennifer Shelton
Elea Sherrod
Deborah Shields
Karen Shird
Deborah Short
Deondra Short
Sheron Sidbury
Randy Simmers
Frances Simms

John Simms
Dawn Simon
Santana Simpson
Robert Smalls
Deborah Smith
Jeannette Smith
Kevin Smith
Marilyn Snow
Elba Solis
Merlyn Solomon
William Spady III
Brady Speers
Owen Spendlove
Will Stanley
Amy Steward
Louasia Stewart
Narjah Stewart
Samuel St-Phard
Renee Stroman
Benjamin Surprin
Loretto Sweeney
Idris Talib
Rene Tameghi
Peter Tang
Victorine Tange
George Tarpeh
Harold Tarrer
Edwin Tatah
Norman Tatum
Eddie Taylor

Edward Taylor
William Tayman
Cynthia Temple
Reginald Tennyson
Fon Tenya
Lolita Terrell
Buhnange Terrence
Sedrick Terry
Johnny Theodore
Arthur Thomas
Barry Thomas
David Thomas
Charlotte Thomason
Monique Thomason
Denise Thompson
Ernest Thompson
Sarah Thompson
Jeannette Thompson-Terry
Samuel Ticha
Diane Tolbert
Tiemoko Toure
Faye Townsend
William Tredway
Kwabena Tuffour
Courtney Turner
David Turner
Donald Turner
Shannon Turner
Dianne Tyler
Alice Tyson

Veronica Udoh
Ejekwu Ugbor
Ngozi Ugbor
William Ugwu
Robyn Underwood
Jennifer Upton
Egwuatu Uradu
Norma Valle
Elaine Vassell-Bango
Patricia Veney
Garth Vickers
Oscar Vigil
James Vivio
Horace Wade
Francina Wade-McQueen
Winston Waite
Jerome Waliszewski
Delroy Walker
Quentin Walker
Rene Walker
Russell Walker
Gilda Wallace
Anne Walters
Jason Walters
Evalyne Ward
Lisa Watkins
Dirk Watters
Derrick Watts
Denise Webb
James Weber

Special Recognition

Peter Wegmann
Artez West
Ashley Williams
Brisha Williams
Christopher Williams
Francine Williams
Gerald Williams
Keshay Williams
Robert Williams
Shante Williams
Lisa Willis
Sydney Willoughby
Danuta Wilson
Jamie Wilson
Jason Wilson
Marinda Wilson
Isaac Wilson, III

Nikki Winkler
James Wise
Janelle Wise
Bryan Wisnewski
Trent Wojtacha
Stephen Woolley
Antoinette Wright
Benjamin Wright
Everett Wright
Farrah Wright
James Wright
Jevauhn Wright
Matthew Yang
Eric Yarbough
Liliana Yee
Sheraton Yee
Karen Young